The Emergent Years

The

George Morrison

Emergent Years

Independent Ireland 1922∗62

GILL AND MACMILLAN

PUBLISHED IN IRELAND BY
GILL AND MACMILLAN LTD
GOLDENBRIDGE
DUBLIN 8
WITH ASSOCIATED COMPANIES IN
AUCKLAND, DALLAS, DELHI, HONG KONG,
JOHANNESBURG, LAGOS, LONDON, MANZINI,
MELBOURNE, NAIROBI, NEW YORK, SINGAPORE,
TOKYO, WASHINGTON
© GEORGE MORRISON, 1984
7171 1341 8
PRINT ORIGINATION IN IRELAND BY KEYWRITE LTD, DUBLIN
PRINTED IN HONG KONG

DESIGNED BY JARLATH HAYES

Introduction

This is a pictorial record of social and cultural life in independent Ireland from the foundation of the state in 1922 to the opening of the national television service forty years later. It was a period of national adolescence. A people who had for generations sought political independence had it in their grasp at last. Not surprisingly, it produced a growing introspection, a turning away from the wider cosmopolitan world associated with the former imperial power.

It is this sense of cultural isolation that strikes the observer most forcefully when he contemplates the period. This tendency was reinforced by the particular circumstances which formed the cultural perspective of the new state. Socially and economically, Ireland was an extremely underdeveloped — indeed in some places backward — country. Its political revolution had not been accompanied by a corresponding radicalism in social thinking. The new Irish establishment was deeply conservative. Freed from the necessity of having to operate in the wider cultural milieu of the old United Kingdom, it now had a free rein to give concrete expression to its more reactionary instincts. The speed and enthusiasm with which the new state passed legislation forbidding divorce and establishing an elaborate system of censorship for books and films are merely the most salient and visible manifestations of the new puritanism. Ironically, nationalism had become the vehicle for a particularly petty form of provincialism.

In one sense, the story of our period is successively that of the establishment of a system of cultural prohibitions, followed by a gradual but increasing process of criticism, and finally, thanks to the unstoppable development of technology, their partial subversion. It is right that this book should end with the establishment of the national television service for, more than anything else, the ubiquity of television destroyed the basis of the old system.

But overall, it is the sense of timelessness that most impresses itself on the mind when one considers Ireland in the first generation after independence. There were changes, certainly, and these are reflected in the photographs and text of this book; but they were neither fundamental nor wide ranging. The period had a quite remarkable cultural homogeneity.

The illustrative material for the book has been assembled from a large variety of sources and not a little has required considerable preparation to render it fit for use. Private collections, the archives of semi-state bodies and newspaper files have contributed to forming the body of the illustrations. The most important contribution from the private collections has been placed at the writer's disposal by the kindness of the Society of Jesus. It is the work of a very remarkable member of that Order, Father Frank Browne.

Nephew of the Most Reverend Robert Browne, Bishop of Cloyne, Father Browne was born in Cork on 3 January 1880. His education was begun at Belvedere College and continued at Castleknock. He entered the noviceship at Tullabeg in 1897. At the completion of his noviceship and a period at the Royal University, he spent three years studying philosophy at Chieri, in Italy, before commencing to teach at Belvedere and Clongowes. During the next seven years, most of which were spent at Belvedere, outside his occupation as a teacher, he founded a bicycling club and a camera club. His interest in photography was to persist throughout his life and has resulted in one of the most important bodies of photographs, the work of a single individual, to be found in the Republic of Ireland, extending, as it does, from the early years of the century until the 1950s. It encompasses both Irish and overseas material including a series of photographs taken on board the S.S. *Titanic*, between Cherbourg and Cobh, at the start of her disastrous maiden voyage.

He was ordained in July 1915, and the following year became chaplain to the Irish Guards, with whom he served in France and Flanders, being wounded several times but returning each time to the front. Besides being frequently mentioned in dispatches, he was awarded the Military Cross and the Belgian Croix de Guerre. He began his tertianship at Tullabeg and continued it at Belvedere College, after which he was appointed Superior of St Francis Xavier's, Gardiner Street, Dublin, where he remained for six years until, for reasons of health, he was sent on a visit to Australia. Returning from Australia in 1928, he was appointed to the mission staff of the Irish Province of the Order.

Throughout the years that followed, a camera was constantly with him and continued constantly in use.

His work entailed much travelling and brought him into touch with all levels of Irish life, thus giving his collection of photographs an exceptional interest from the point of view of social history. It also contains much of architectural and antiquarian interest as well as many interiors, both humble and grand, while his love of children is especially demonstrated by his many fine and spontaneous photographs of them which are a recurrent theme throughout his many years of work. He died in 1960, in his eighty-first year.

I am greatly indebted to the Abbey Theatre for their help in making available a number of unique photographs which enable me to illustrate the styles of theatrical presentation and the effects of what might be called cross-fertilisation, particularly in the 1930s.

Without the exceedingly generous assistance of Richard Pine, I could hardly have hoped to present an impression of the influence of the Dublin Gate Theatre during its most creative years. The patient and meticulous work which he has given, over the years, to this subject must inevitably leave all successors much in his debt. My particular thanks are due to Carolyn Swift for the trouble she has taken at a very busy period to provide me with invaluable visual material with which to illustrate the importance of the Pike Theatre Club in the 1950s.

I should like also to thank Radio Telefís Éireann, the *Irish Times* and the *Irish Press* for their assistance and, particularly, Mitchell Cogley for the trouble he has taken to make available to me a photograph without which the important place in the cultural life of Ireland of a distinguished and charming lady could not have been visually represented.

GEORGE MORRISON

1
Timothy Healy, first Governor-General of the Irish Free State. A prominent Irish MP at Westminster, he became one of the leaders of the anti-Parnellite faction after the O'Shea divorce case. His name was put forward for the office of Governor-General by the President of the Executive Council of the Provisional Government, W. T. Cosgrave. The same day that the two British parliamentary bills bringing the Irish Free State into being received the royal assent, 5 December 1922, King George V also signed the instrument approving Healy's appointment. The following day, he took up residence in the Vice-Regal Lodge, Phoenix Park, left vacant at the departure of the last Lord Lieutenant, Viscount Fitzalan, nearly a year previously. On the same day the Dáil met and, with the absence of all Republican supporters but with the presence of Labour Party TDs, the members of the Senate were elected. Governor-General Healy performed his first public function by convening the Senate on 9 December. Three days later, at a meeting of both houses, he read the king's speech; all Labour Party TDs left the house in protest and did not return until the departure of the Governor-General. Under the terms of the Government of Ireland Act, 1920, the Provisional Government had become the government of the Irish Free State.

2
General Richard Mulcahy and Mr Ernest Blythe, on the occasion of the founding of the Cumann na nGaedheal Party. Taking its name from the association established by Arthur Griffith in 1900, which had come to an end with the foundation of Sinn Féin in 1905, the Cumann na nGaedheal political party was called into being in April 1923 and, due to the abstentionist policies of Republican TDs and the small number of Labour Party representatives elected, it was enabled to pursue its policies without effective opposition for almost four years, until Fianna Fáil TDs took their seats in the Dáil in 1927. As Chief of Staff of the Pro-Treaty forces in the Civil War following the death of Michael Collins, General Mulcahy was appointed Minister for Defence, a position he was to hold only for a short while until his resignation following the army mutiny of 1924, although he returned to the Executive Council in 1927. Ernest Blythe had commenced his cabinet career under the Provisional Government in 1922 as Minister for Local Government. On Collins's death he accepted the appointment of Minister for Finance. It was in the latter capacity that he was among the signatories of the 'ultimate financial agreement' with Great Britain on 3 December 1925.

3

3
Kevin O'Higgins, Vice-President of the Executive Council (a position roughly corresponding to that of Tanaiste today), was considered to be the 'strong man' of Cumann na nGaedheal. Under the Provisional Government he had been one of the most determined supporters of the execution of selected Republican prisoners after sentencing by courts martial, during the Civil War. It was he who as Minister for Home Affairs introduced into the Dáil the legislation for film censorship and this at a time when the Civil War was still in progress. The bill had its second reading on 10 May 1923. Much of the debate makes comical reading today, but it is of interest to note that among the chief pressure groups lobbying for the enactment of film censorship were the Irish Vigilance Association, the Priests' Social Guild, the Catholic Church in Ireland, the Protestant Episcopalian Church in Ireland and the Presbyterian Church. It was only following the approaches of these groups that local government

bodies joined in the call for the imposition of censorship. However, the negative response of the Cumann na nGaedheal administration to the great new art of the twentieth century was not confined to censorship. In its embryonic condition in a new state, while it was struggling hard to find its feet in native production, the only recognition it was to receive officially was the imposition of taxation as well as censorship! No positive encouragement of any kind was given to what was to become, as the motion picture arts of film and television, the chief medium of mass communication. Indeed, the almost incredible lack of awareness of its vast cultural and educational potential was coupled with a narrow-minded fear of what the new medium might bring, and led successive Irish administrations into a pattern of negative thought which effectively prevented them from exploiting the potential of the motion-picture arts for decades to come.

4

4

A solitary voice only was raised in the Dáil to question the wisdom of the film censorship bill, that of Thomas Johnson, leader of the Labour Party. 'I doubt', he said, 'whether you could choose one man, or even a small board of appeal, who will not be extravagantly puritanical or, on the other hand, careless, and whose conceptions of morality and social order are too narrow and perhaps old-fashioned. It is rather a risky undertaking.' Later in his speech he pointed out that the wording of the conclusion of Section 7, sub-section 2 could be used to authorise the film censor to apply a political censorship and his objection led to the dropping of the objectionable phrase. The contribution of Professor Magennis to the debate epitomised the complacency with which the Cumann na nGaedheal party as a whole received the bill. He began by seeking to brush aside Thomas Johnson's dissent. 'This is one of the few bills', he said, 'for which I expected absolute unanimity. I think, notwithstanding the speech of Deputy Johnson, we may regard him as supporting the measure ...' He provided, further on, what seems to a modern reader to be an illuminating example of the prevailing psychological climate of the new Irish legislature:

There is the flapper and the corresponding youth — two lovers. The invariable end of the story is, they elope in a motor car, pursued by the police scouts, who are observing not that they are breaking the moral code or the moral conventions, but that they are breaking the laws with regard to the speed limit. They are not fast, I should say, in the moral sense. That is why the public are not aware that the thing is objectionable in its influence. They always find an obliging clergyman or Justice of the Peace round the corner.... If Eddie So-and-So and Mabel Something-Else may do such things, and if it is not wrong in their case, why should it be wrong in ours? The whole idea of parental control, all that we associate with the sacredness not merely of matriomony, but of the associations leading up to it, are sapped by those things.

Later he was to give utterance to two amazing statements:

There is not a boy or girl of 14 or 16 years of age who need not at the end of a year be a past-master in every detail of every form of vicious life in every quarter of the globe by merely going through this education of weekly *seances* in one of our most respectable cinemas.

Complaining that the penalties envisaged in the act were inadequate he exclaimed:

The penalty is not enough. I might be thought a fanatic in the matter, otherwise I would propose that anyone fined repeatedly for these offences should be deprived of citizenship altogether.

5

5
Inishmaan Post Office, Aran Islands, Co. Galway. Just before the signs in Irish were put up there. After the War of Independence and devastation of the Civil War, the Irish Free State had to face the appalling prospect of a ruined economy and devastated communications. Living conditions, particularly in the south and west and in the urban slums, were truly dreadful. Changing name signs was relatively easy, however, and was put in hand at once.

6.
In the areas that were to become the Gaeltachts, conditions in 1923 were unbelievably primitive. Although many Nationalist enthusiasts showed a certain sentimental nostalgia for such ways of life, those who had to experience them as their year-round environment were never slow to take any opportunity to improve them.

6

7

In the effort to get the economy of the Free State into operation, first priority had to be given to the restoration of communications. Here President Cosgrave drives the first train across the repaired section of Mallow railway bridge, destroyed in the Civil War. But the event, which took place in September 1923, savours rather of a propaganda exercise for, as will be seen from the photograph, the bridge did not yet actually extend across the river!

7

The Free State was very unlucky with the weather
conditions which prevailed for the first couple of years
of its history. An unusually wet period resulted in
waterlogged land, handicapping the farming
community's struggle to recover from the economic
depression and the depredations of war. The continued
heavy rainfalls culminated in the great floods of
January 1924 on the Nore, Blackwater and Shannon.

8

9

Barry Fitzgerald as 'Captain' Boyle in Sean O'Casey's
Juno and the Paycock. The curfews of the 'Black and
Tan' period and the disruption of civil war imposed
crippling conditions on theatre in Ireland. Still without
a subsidy, struggling on from production to production
and getting more and more into debt, the Abbey
Theatre was reluctantly inclined to put on more and
more popular kitchen comedies, which attracted good
houses, in order to keep its head above water. In the
spring of 1923 it put on a play of a different and very
topical character by an unknown young playwright:
The Shadow of a Gunman. It was at once apparent
that a new genius had arrived, who was doing for the
urban proletariat what J. M. Synge had done for the
country people of the West. It was an immediate
success and was revived at the start of the next season,
when it ran to full houses. On 3 March 1924, Sean
O'Casey's next play was given its first performance.
Juno and the Paycock ran for two weeks to packed
houses and was revived in August to equal acclaim. In
June 1924, however, when the play moved to Cork, the
theatre management insisted that Mary Boyle's
pregnancy be altered to tuberculosis! Fortunately, the
pressure to do so was resisted.

9

10

10

F. J. McCormick as 'Joxer' Daly. These wonderful
plays, which were to raise Sean O'Casey to the status
of a world-famous writer, infused a new life into the
Abbey actors and greatly restored the morale of the
theatre. Lady Gregory wrote after a performance of
Juno: 'This is one of the evenings at the Abbey that
makes me glad to have been born.' Nevertheless, in
spite of the popularity of the O'Casey plays, the
theatre was still in dire financial straits. In the summer
of 1924, Yeats, Lady Gregory, Lennox Robinson and
the other directors considered handing the theatre over
to the Free State government but in the following year,
with the support of Ernest Blythe, Desmond FitzGerald
and Eoin MacNeill and with further encouragement
from Thomas Johnson, it was given an annual subsidy
and has had one ever since.

11

Athenry Agricultural School, Athenry, Co. Galway, April 1924: pupils learning to survey land and take levels. There was a great need to encourage the spread of scientific farming methods in Ireland. The World War and the subsequent disturbances in the country had meant that agricultural technology and education had fallen far behind even other small European countries such as Denmark. The farming strategies of the nineteenth century had been geared to supplying the British market with primary products; this pattern was to change only very slowly indeed and hardly at all under the Free State.

12

In May 1924 the Free State appointed its new judges. Here President Cosgrave chats to General Tom Ennis as they arrive at Dublin Castle, two members of the Dublin Metropolitan Police at their side.

11

12

13

13
Court officials assembling at Dublin Castle for the
new Justices to take their oath of allegiance to the
crown in the presence of the Governor-General,
Timothy Healy.

14

Among the women imprisoned in Kilmainham Jail was Grace Plunkett, née Gifford, who had married Joseph Plunkett in that same prison the night before his execution in 1916. During her captivity she painted this sketch on the wall of her cell.

15

By the spring of 1924 the Cosgrave administration felt sufficiently secure to begin releasing most of the 15,000 Civil War prisoners that were then in jails and prison-camps throughout the country. It is an eloquent expression of the differences that characterised the Irish and Spanish Civil Wars and the regimes that succeeded them that such an open and humane action could be taken by the Free State. Some Republican prisoners were still held and others imprisoned before the general release of 1932; nevertheless, the freeing of 15,000 prisoners so soon after the cessation of hostilities must be considered unique among the civil wars of this century. There were some hundreds of women among those released.

14

15

16

On 15 August 1924, de Valera, released a few days previously, returned to Ennis, Co. Clare. He got a tumultuous welcome from a multitude assembled from all over the West of Ireland and addressed them, beginning: 'As I was saying when I was interrupted ...' It was to be the beginning of the course that would return him to power.

16

17

That same summer of 1924 saw a young and relatively unknown Irish artist and actor from Cork city play his first part in an Irish drama: Micheál mac Liammóir. He took a leading part in the Irish-produced film *Land of her Fathers*. The film had a cast of many leading contemporary Irish actors. Later that year, the only copy was stolen in New York and to this day has never been seen again.

17

Royal Ulster Constabulary and B Specials on the
border near Newry, Co. Down, in an attempt to
prevent Eamon de Valera, a constitutionally nominated
candidate for the seat of South Down in the British
general election, from attending an election meeting at
Newry on 24 November 1924. He had been prohibited
from entering Northern Ireland under an order of the
government of Northern Ireland signed by the Minister
for Home Affairs, Dawson Bates. The border with
Northern Ireland had become very real, though
impossible to close, as it remains today. De Valera
succeeded in slipping across, in spite of the
considerable forces mobilised against him, but was
arrested at Newry Town Hall before he could address
his constituents.

18

19

Mr Justice Feetham, of the South African magistracy, the chairman of the Boundary Commission which was given the task of adjusting the border between the Free State and Northern Ireland.

19

20

The three members of the Boundary Commission, shortly after they had begun their work in December 1924. Due to intransigence on both sides, the Commission achieved nothing of substance and it did not last long. Thus were dashed the hopes of many supporters of the Free State as well as those expressed by the late Michael Collins. On Mr Justice Feetham's immediate left is the Northern Ireland representative, J. R. Fisher of the Unionist Party; on his left is Professor Eoin MacNeill, the representative of the Cumann na nGaedheal government of the Free State. He was Minister for Education in that government and this reminds one that a great opportunity was lost, at the establishment of the Free State, of abolishing that pattern of religious segregation in primary and secondary education that had been inherited from the British administration.

20

21

In 1925 the Shannon Scheme, one of the most important developments in the history of the State, was commenced. Although some thought it over-ambitious at the time, it proved to be one of the most significant advances in the development of the Irish economy. One of the most alarming discoveries of the early years of the Free State was that private capital simply had no interest in engaging, on its own account, in the scale of investment needed to provide the basic industrial structures necessary to the country. The most important of these was electric power. A great generating scheme based on the Shannon, the longest river in the British Isles, augmented by the natural reservoir of Lough Derg, had been a dream too ambitious to tempt even the strongest combinations of private financial institutions; the more so as the large sums involved would have to be deployed over many years and the recouping of the investment would take many years more. Faced with this situation, the Free State government stepped in and work began on 13 August 1925.

21

On 1 January 1926, the Gaelic writer and scholar Dr Douglas Hyde inaugurated the national radio service, Radio Éireann. It broadcast from a tiny studio in Little Denmark Street, near the GPO, from where the signal went, by land-line, to the one kilowatt Marconi transmitter at McKee barracks near the Phoenix Park, a power output equivalent to one bar of an ordinary domestic electric fire. The entire staff of the station, including the chief announcer Máiréad ní Ghráda, comprised a mere five people, not including the radio orchestra, which consisted of a quartet! But for the fact that the contracts of the quartet were not completed until a little after the opening of the station, Radio Éireann or 2 RN as the call sign of the station was, would have been the first radio service in the world to have an orchestra: as it was, the Danish radio service just beat Ireland for this honour. The Cork station, call sign 6 CK, officially opened on 26 April 1926, but did not begin regular transmissions until 30 April. When recorded music was played over 2 RN, this was provided by a clockwork-driven accoustic gramophone, placed near the all-purpose microphone. There was no statutory instrument providing for censorship of the new medium, but the need for this was obviated by a most stringently applied self-censorship, so that an atmosphere of the uttermost decorum prevailed. This was applied very intensely. The present writer's father, who had a particularly clear speaking voice, was, in the very early days, asked to read some fairy stories for children. All went splendidly until the script for the last of the series arrived back from the surveillance of the directorate. The story was 'The Emperor's New Clothes' and a broad dark blue pencil had been drawn firmly through the word 'naked' wherever it appeared and a superscription added for use in its place: 'dressed only in a simple white singlet.' My father remonstrated, in vain, that there was no possible way of telling the story with this absurd substitution, but the powers that were were adamant. It ended his interest in participating in Irish radio.

22

23

23

Barry Fitzgerald as 'Fluther' Good in *The Plough and the Stars*. One of the greatest actors that the Irish theatre has produced, Fitzgerald was soon to be lost to Dublin due to his remarkable success as a film actor. Some of his finest performances on the screen are to be seen in the films of John Ford, particularly his little known but greatest artistic achievement, *Long Voyage Home*, adapted from three of the 'sea' plays of Eugene O'Neill, in which Fitzgerald plays the 'donkey-man'. A donkey-engine was an auxilliary engine found on steamships.

24

On 8 February 1926, Sean O'Casey's third play opened at the Abbey. Within four days it was the occasion of riotous scenes at the theatre that recalled Synge's *Playboy of the Western World*. The set for the first act of *The Plough and the Stars* reminds us today of a particular aspect of the Abbey's ethos. It was a theatre with a singularly literary character, which could hardly be the occasion of surprise when one considers the composition of the theatre's board of directors. The ideas, the dialogue and the playing of the actors were the heart of the presentation; the visual elements of the production were much less important. Set design and stage utilisation, in a visual sense, were exceedingly primitive. The general format of presentations was a conventional 'fourth wall' theatre with a quasi-naturalistic, rather symmetrically arranged 'box' set. Ill-fitting flats and other careless visual details were commonplace. Windows and doors were unconvincing and very little imagination was shown in the use of light, even when one makes allowance for the rather simple lighting equipment in the theatre at that time. Today, we can see these things very clearly in the photographs of the Abbey stage and sets of the 1920s and early 1930s. This visual unawareness, a characteristic of much Irish life of the period, meant that the work of Gordon Craig had little impact on the Abbey's presentations; and it was soon to be a factor in the theatre's failure to comprehend the later work of O'Casey himself.

24

25.
The set for Act II of *The Plough and the Stars* in its first production, 8 February 1926. The occasion of the riot which took place on the evening of Thursday, 11 February was the bringing of the Irish Volunteer and Citizen Army flags into the pub from a meeting supposed to have taken place outside, an incident expressive of the real honesty and down-to-earth authenticity of O'Casey's writing and characterisation. All accounts corroborate the fact that the riot was a deplorable exhibition of thoughtless chauvinism, a feature of Irish life that does emerge from time to time. It was the first sign that many elements in Irish life were not yet ready to accept O'Casey as the great artist which he was. The actors continued playing for as long as they could. Ria Mooney, playing the part of the prostitute, Rosie Redmond, was actually pelted with lumps of coal; (imagine members of the Irish Volunteers being shown in the same pub as a prostitute!). Yeats, as he had been before during the *Playboy* riot, was magnificent. Speaking to the audience (and to the press) he said: 'I thought you had got tired of this, which commenced fifteen years ago. But you have disgraced yourselves again. Is this going to be a recurring celebration of Irish genius? Synge first and then O'Casey. The news of the happening in the last few minutes here will flash from country to country. Dublin has again rocked the cradle of a reputation.'

25

23

A little later in the year, Sean O'Casey went to London, where he married the actress Eileen Carey. It was to be a long and very happy marriage. Lack of understanding of his work was to discourage his permanent return to Ireland.

26

27

There were other mass spectacles which received a more general acceptance from the Irish public. On 20 March 1926, a memorial to the fourteen spectators of a Gaelic football match indiscriminately shot by RIC Auxilliaries in 1920, was unveiled on the Cusack stand, Croke Park. Even the subject of Gaelic sport, however, has not always been devoid of controversy!

28

The year 1926 saw the first English translation of the great Gaelic eighteenth-century satirical poem, Brian Merriman's *The Midnight Court*, by a new young writer from Co. Waterford, Percival Arland Ussher, who was to continue writing both in Irish and English and become one of Ireland's leading philosophers.

28

27

29
Flower-sellers at the Nelson Pillar, Dublin, 1920s. During the eighteenth and early nineteenth century, before the establishment of railways, the stage-coaches from various parts of the country terminated their journeys in O'Connell Street, at that time known by its earlier name of Sackville Street. The street was then, and even until after the Second World War, very much more the the hub of Dublin than it is today. The advent of the city tramways, first horse-drawn and later electric, left a small open space free at the base of the Nelson Pillar which was a highly prized position for fruit and flower sellers. Our overcrowded petrol and diesel traffic, as well as the prohibition of their right to use the site in 1927 and finally the physical destruction of the pillar itself, have deprived us of this pleasant amenity.

30
Madame Markievicz, de Valera and Mrs Tom Clarke, after the meeting which founded the Fianna Fáil party in April 1926. At the time that this picture was taken, Constance Markievicz's health was failing rapidly and, only a matter of weeks later, this great-hearted, brave and compassionate woman, who had been so much loved by the urban working class of Dublin in particular, was dead.

30

31
It was impossible for the Cumann na nGaedheal administration ever to feel really secure and preoccupations with defence were never far from the President's thoughts. Extensive army manoeuvres were held in counties Wicklow and Carlow in the late summer of 1926. Here, watched by the then Minister for Defence, President Cosgrave takes a sight during artillery practice in the Glen of Imaal.

31

32

33

32

Meanwhile the huge undertaking of the Shannon Scheme continued, largely in the hands of German contractors though employing considerable local labour. Enormous digging and earth-moving machinery was now at work, chiefly on the excavation and building-up of a canal that would draw off the necessarily very large volume of water from the Shannon at a point a little south of Killaloe and deliver it to the intakes of the penstocks of the power house that was being built at Ardnacrusha, a little north west of Limerick City, in Co. Clare.

33

Never before in Ireland had such a vast quantity of earth been moved in such a comparatively short time and the extra employment given is still remembered in the area.

34

Early in 1927, President Cosgrave, with the help of several labourers, turned the windlass that raised the first pylon of the two main high-tension power lines of the early stage of the scheme. They ran from Ardnacrusha to Dublin and to Cork.

35

Surmounted by a young fir tree and festooned in greenery, the German-designed pylon looks like a maypole erected for some pagan fertility ceremony.

35

34

35a

35A

Ministers for Finance are rarely popular at Budget time and Ernest Blythe was no exception in March 1927. *Dublin Opinion's* cartoon was to gain further point later when Blythe's refusal to surrender his pistol at the request of the de Valera administration became a *cause célèbre*. An additional ironical twist was lent too by the Minister's growing dislike of the works of Sean O'Casey.

36

President Cosgrave called a general election in June 1927 and, at this election, besides the Labour Party and the recently formed Fianna Fáil, two other new parties were to contend against Cumann na nGaedheal. These were the Farmers' Party, later to be known as the Centre Party (though in fact being somewhat right of centre in character as events were to show) and the National League. The latter party had been called into being by Captain W. A. Redmond, son of John Redmond, the post-Parnell leader of the Irish Parliamentary Party of Westminister days. In the extreme south east, particularly in the vicinity of Wexford town, there was a strong loyalty to the Redmond family which brought considerable crowds to Captain Redmond's election meetings there in early June.

37

Captain William Redmond addressing his Wexford constituents on behalf of the National League party. His campaign met with a modest regional success. Eight National League candidates were returned to the Dáil.

36

38

The election result was very unsettling for Cumann na nGaedheal because they were now reduced to only forty-seven votes in the new chamber, even counting the vote of the Ceann Comhairle, who had as usual been returned unopposed. With a most decided success for such a newly formed party, Fianna Fáil had taken forty-four and, shortly after the new session began, their number was augmented by one of the independents. With twenty-two Labour seats, eleven Farmers' Party, eight National League and ten of the remaining independents, there seemed a good chance of overturning the government with a possibility of a coalition led by Fianna Fáil, but the problem remained of getting the Fianna Fáil deputies past the oath to the crown and seated in the house. After taking extensive legal advice, the opinion was given that, under the terms of the Treaty, an oath to the crown was not obligatory before the election of the new Ceann Comhairle brought about the constitution of the house; before that any deputies could attend and vote for whatever TD they chose as Ceann Comhairle. On 23 June, the opening day of the new session, de Valera led his elected deputies into Leinster House to test this means of restoring open elective democracy.

37

40

41

39
Press reporters and photographers crowd around the entrance to Leinster House after the Fianna Fáil deputies have entered to take their seats before the election of the new Ceann Comhairle.

40
All of the Fianna Fáil TDs were barred from the chamber, bringing about a continued stalemate over the question of the oath to the crown. Immediately after the episode, de Valera made a speech to the Fianna Fáil supporters who had gathered in considerable numbers in Dawson Street. He addressed them from a window above the shop belonging to a leading member of Fianna Fáil.

41
A crowd of Fianna Fáil supporters listening to his speech.

42
On 10 July 1927, Kevin O'Higgins, Vice-President of
the Executive Council, was shot dead by two IRA men.
The killing was not the result of a policy decision by
the IRA Army Council and no orders for his shooting
had been given. It appears that it was yet another
example of the terrible bitterness remaining over from
the more deplorable incidents of the Civil War which
still affected many sincere and still disenfranchised
young Irish people who clung to the ideal of the
uncompromised Republic even when the possibility of
practically achieving that republic had been lost. Nor
was it by any means the only or the last incident of its
kind either before or after 1927. It had immediate and
important political consequences which were to bring
about a further alienation of the IRA and its
supporters from the mainstream of Irish political life.
Cumann na nGaedheal immediately introduced three
draconian bills, which, in the absence of the Fianna
Fáil deputies from the chamber, it was readily able to
pass. One of these cut off the possibility of abolishing,
by means of a referendum, the oath which barred the
Fianna Fáil deputies from the chamber. A second
declared all seats vacant if not taken up within a
period of two months from the commencement of a
Dáil, while the third gave the government stringent

43

emergency powers which abrogated the normal protection in law of citizens. The murder of O'Higgins could only benefit political reaction.

43
Thomas Johnson, leader of the Parliamentary Labour Party, and other Labour TDs, at the entrance to Leinster House. The state of the parties in the new Dáil and the likelihood of the Fianna Fáil deputies taking their seats gave Labour a hope that, with their twenty-two seats, they might be able to form an alliance which could bring about a change of government to a coalition in which Labour policies might begin to have some influence. Talks were opened with Fianna Fáil, who also began discussions with Redmond's National League, but the plan never came to fruition. With time rapidly running out under the new Electoral Amendment Bill, Fianna Fáil had to arrive at some formula which would enable them to take their seats in the Dáil before they became vacant again under the act. On 11 July, de Valera, on behalf of the Parliamentary Party as a whole, declared to the Clerk of the Dáil that he was not taking any Oath and signed the book presented to him by Colm Ó Murchadha for signature. The other Fianna Fáil TDs

followed suit and, taking their places in the chamber, brought about a fundamental change in the Irish political scene.

44
TDs entering Leinster House, 1927. On 16 August, Thomas Johnson moved a vote of 'no confidence' in the government. But for the absence of one of the National League members, John Jinks from Sligo, the Cumann na nGaedheal government would have fallen. It was plain that the government position was now untenable, and a few days later President Cosgrave called for the dissolution of the Dáil and another general election. The snap election which followed was characterised by a strong denunciation of Fianna Fáil by a great many Roman Catholic priests as well as by supporters of Cumann na nGaedheal, while the latter were also supported by those of Unionist sympathies. In spite of this, Fianna Fáil gained thirteen more seats than it had won in June. Cumann na nGaedheal gained fifteen more and the other parties were the losers, particularly Labour, which was reduced to eight seats. Cumann na nGaedheal was able to remain in office but with Fianna Fáil as the main opposition party.

44

45

46

45
Following the death of Timothy Healy, James MacNeill
was installed as the second Governor-General of the
Irish Free State in January 1928. Brother of Eoin
MacNeill, he had previously held the office of High
Commissioner for the Irish Free State in London.

46
The MacNeills on their way from government buildings
to the Vice-Regal Lodge, Phoenix Park.

47
Governor-General and Lady Josephine MacNeill at the
Vice-Regal Lodge.

47

48
Micheál mac Liammóir and Hilton Edwards.
Throughout the summer of 1927, mac Liammóir had
been touring with Anew McMaster's company, as he
had decided to give up his career as a painter and
illustrator for the stage. At Enniscorthy, Co. Wexford,
one of the actors was taken ill and was replaced by a
young actor from London, Hilton Edwards. The
meeting of mac Liammóir and Edwards was to have
great significance for the development of theatre in
Dublin. It soon became apparant that their ideas on
theatre dove-tailed in an exceptionally creative way. In
the cold month of February 1928, during a second
McMaster tour, the idea of starting a new theatre in
Dublin crystallised into a determination. Coralie
Carmichael, an actress who was to play so prominent a
part in that theatre, was with them as they discussed
their plans at a small country pub in Co. Tipperary.

49
In April, a most unusual aeroplane flew into Baldonnel,
the Air Corps aerodrome near Dublin. It was one of
the world's very first all-metal aircraft and it was on a
quite exceptional mission, nothing less than an attempt
to make the very first non-stop east-to-west crossing
of the Atlantic Ocean by aeroplane. On board were
Baron Guenther von Huenefeld and Captain Herman
Köhl. Mechanics at Baldonnel worked around the clock
to get the aircraft in readiness. The photograph shows
the characteristic corrugated metal skin used to give
rigidity and strength, a typical feature of Junkers-built
aeroplanes of the period. When she took off for her
successful crossing, she carried a third man, Major
James Fitzmaurice of the Free State Army.

49

50
Major James Fitzmaurice and Captain Herman Köhl
enjoy what must have been a very sweet-tasting
cigarette after their Atlantic crossing to Greenly Island,
Newfoundland. They were brought by dog sleigh from
the icy country where the Bremen landed, out of fuel,
to a small air-field where they could be picked up by
the aircraft in the background. They went on to a
ticker-tape reception in New York.

50

51

Madame D. Bannard-Cogley. When Hilton Edwards arrived in Dublin, in the spring of 1928, to commence his work of getting an entirely new theatre into functional operation, one of his most valuable helpers was 'Toto' Cogley. She was a wonderful, dynamic, warm-hearted tiny French woman, married inalienably to the culture of Dublin, but bringing to it the exciting breath of European art and thought. Her cabaret, 'The Studio Theatre Club', was as much a small experimental theatre as a cabaret and she encouraged young actors, painters, sculptors and musicians to work at their projects there, giving them a chance to form creative ensembles not available with the same freedom painters, sculptors and musicians to work at their projects there, giving them a chance to form creative ensembles not available with the same freedom elsewhere. Her ready imagination was at once fired by

the possibility and the necessity of a new theatre in Dublin, which would look outwards to the world. She and Gearóid O'Lochlainn, the actor, set about mobilising their contacts to get a fund-raising operation under way. 'Toto' Cogley, Gearóid O'Lochlainn, Micheál mac Liammóir and Hilton Edwards were to become the founder directors of the Dublin Gate Theatre Company. She remained a director for the rest of her life.

52

It was around this time that, after several rejected designs, Micheál mac Liammóir drew the final form of the Dublin Gate Theatre colophon, which was to become as famous as that of the Abbey Theatre. But before the Gate Theatre Studio project, as it was first called, could advance any further, another had to be set up. Professor Liam Ó Briain of Galway arranged

40

for mac Liammóir and Edwards to lend their expertise to the establishment of the first subsidised entirely Gaelic theatre in the world, the Taibhdhearc na Gaillimhe. This gave mac Liammóir the chance to produce, with Hilton Edwards, the Gaelic play that he had written in 1925, 'Diarmuid agus Gráinne', in which he himself played Diarmuid to Máire ní Scolaidhe's Gráinne.

53
Near Limerick, the scene in the neighbourhood of Ardnacrusha had been transformed. Giant machines of steel and timber, running on special railway tracks and looking like enormous constructivist theatre sets, were continuously making and pouring concrete as the dam and canal were reaching their final stages.

54
Creeping along its rails like a huge prehistoric monster, but ten times larger, a chain bucket profiling machine adjusts the slope of the canal bank to exactly the right angle before it is lined with concrete.

53

54

55

Entrance to the Peacock Theatre, just prior to its demolition. On Sunday 14 October 1928, the Peacock Theatre opened its doors to a momentous event in the history of Irish theatre. On a minute stage (only eighteen inches above the level of the auditorium floor, twenty-four feet wide and only nine and a half feet deep), the Dublin Gate Theatre Studio were about to present the most elaborate and, in its settings, one of the most diversified plays of the great Norwegian playwright, Henrik Ibsen, *Peer Gynt*.

56

The stage of the Peacock Theatre, just prior to its demolition. The sheer imaginative boldness and confidence born of a real knowledge of stage technique enabled the Gate to bring off this extraordinary *tour de force*. It did so on a stage so tiny and in a theatre so small (only one hundred and one seats) that even a very experienced producer might be pardoned for believing that only the most intimate drama could be possible there. The back wall of the stage was converted so that it could do duty as a cyclorama. Because of the absence of a light-pit at the back of the stage, the lights for illuminating the lower part of the cyclorama had to be masked either by a low rostrum or cut-outs, leaving about four to five feet of stage space for acting between the lights and the line of the proscenium. But the gain in a psychological feeling of depth was tremendous. The actors, using a double reversible pair of black steps, could be thrown against an apparent infinity of space behind. It was a master-stroke, as antithetical to the symmetrical 'fourth wall' box-set of the Abbey tradition as could be imagined.

57

Coralie Carmichael in the title role of Salome in the world's first public production of Oscar Wilde's play. *Salome* opened at the Peacock on 12 December 1928, preceded by a short curtain-raiser by Ereinov.

Peer Gynt had been succeeded by O'Neill's *The Hairy Ape*, which also deployed a style of stagecraft radically different from that to be found at the Abbey — a split level stage, the lower boxed-in part representing the stoke-hold and, above this, an area where the 'on deck' scenes were played. Extremely ingenious lighting differentiated the two environments and allowed an inertia-free transfer, dispensing with the need to lower the curtain. Following upon this, mac Liammóir's translation into English of *Diarmuid and Gráinne* was given and the world première of *Salome* followed. Through mac Liammóir's designs for costume and décor and Edwards' dynamic production and lighting, it was demonstrated beyond doubt that a new, visually orientated theatre had arrived in Ireland.

In 1934, Hilton Edwards wrote:

> 'Here we used not only a definite scheme of design for all the costumes, but a definite scheme of massed colours; black and yellow for the Jews; green and violet for the court, and white for the Roman ambassadors. Herod was dressed in black and silver and green, crowned and entwined with purple roses. The set was a matte black picked out in metallic silver against a sky of jade, and lit with a peculiar peacock-blue-green flood, obtained by an admixture of colours. The dominant positions were picked out in steel-blue, while from the palace the thrones were faintly flushed by a smouldering purple which faded before the moon and became red like blood and glowed in reflection from the silver ornamentations'

56

57

58

58
While the Dublin Gate Theatre were preparing to stage
RUR by Karel Capek, another dramatic event was
being staged in O'Connell Street, Dublin. On the
anniversary of the end of the Easter Rising, President
Cosgrave was re-opening the rebuilt General Post
Office. The thirteenth anniversary of the proclamation
of Irish freedom was to be the occasion of that event
as well as an unusually elaborate Civic Week later in
the year. But the celebration of freedom was not
without its ironies. In 1925, a motion prohibiting civil
divorce had been introduced into the Dáil, thus
disenfranchising all those whose religious convictions
or whose secular morality did not prohibit them from
exercising a right to such a remedy, while, by
introducing the element of compulsion, implied that
those whose creed might prohibit them from taking
such an action would do so if they were given the
chance. But, as though to contradict the affirmation of
freedom represented by the O'Connell Street
ceremony, a bill had just been passed making all
publications subject to a censorship board. Nor was
the sole purpose of this bill the censorship of literature
or the mass media. Written into the text of the bill
was a specific prohibition relating to the publication of

information on the subject of contraceptive techniques.
The dissemination of knowledge on contraception was,
by a peculiarly Irish kind of hypocrisy, to be prohibited
as though it were obscene!

59
Our great poet, W. B. Yeats, had attacked the
Censorship of Publications Bill in the Seanad with all the
vigour and eloquence at his command. He regarded it as
grossly tyrannical and culturally destructive. Sir John
Keane also opposed it to the best of his ability. But there
could be no stopping the passage of the bill and it became
law. Though defeated, Yeats did not let the matter rest;
with the collaboration of George Bernard Shaw, he
organised the founding of a new institution, to give
support to Irish writers: the Irish Academy of Letters.
Speaking on the section of the bill dealing with the
prohibition of the dissemination of information on
contraception, during its second reading in the Dáil, the
Minister for Justice said:

> That section has been attacked by persons who say that the
> question is a social one, and that the merits or demerits
> should be argued out. That is a proposition to which we
> cannot and will not assent. In our views on this matter we

are perfectly clear and perfectly definite. We will not allow, as far as it lies with us to prevent it, the free discussion of this question which entails on one side of it advocacy. We have made up our minds that it is wrong. That conclusion is for us unalterable. We consider it to be a matter of grave importance. We have decided, call it dogmatically if you like — and I believe almost all persons in this country are in agreement with us — that that question shall not be freely and openly discussed.

In a truly remarkable gesture of 'hands across the border' in the cause of political reaction, the member for Trinity College, Sir James Craig, who attended the debate in person, supported the prohibition of books on contraception.

59

60

Model of set for *The Power of Darkness* by Leo Tolstoy, with which the Dublin Gate Theatre Studio opened their second season. Even though it was quite impossible to sustain themselves financially at the tiny Peacock Theatre, Edwards, mac Liammóir and their supporters were convinced of the wisdom of continuing the remaining portion of the lease of the Peacock Theatre with a second season of plays. This extremely poor photograph shows a model for one of the sets of the opening production. It gives no inkling of the eerie feeling given to them by mac Liammóir's sense of colour and Edward's masterly lighting, though those who remember the model set in the foyer of the Gate Theatre can get some impression of their effectiveness.

The second production of the season was David Sears's play on the Anglo-Irish struggle *Juggernaut* and, true to the pattern of presenting national and international drama, this was followed by *The Adding Machine* by Elmer Rice.

60

61

The last play to be staged by the Dublin Gate Theatre Studio at the end of their second season in the Peacock was to give instant success to a new and most original Irish playwright, Denis Johnston. In his play, *The Old Lady Says No*, he examines with objectivity the sentimental and chauvinistic assumptions that had become such clichés of contemporary thought in the Ireland of the immediate post-Civil War years and the Cumann na nGaedheal establishment. Conceived in an expressionist style, an idiom then rarely seen in the Irish professional theatre, it found in Hilton Edwards's brilliant production and mac Liammóir's set and costume design an outstandingly sympathetic realisation that was to become an important part of the Gate Theatre's dramatic repertoire. Like Sean O'Casey's *The Silver Tassie*, *The Old Lady Says No* had been rejected by the Abbey Theatre, and some have seen the change of title from the original *Shadow Dance* as embodying a reference to the reception accorded it by Lady Gregory. Be that as it may, the new title was a very much more appropriate one and its presentation showed, once again, the great cultural advantage of having a permanent alternative theatre in Dublin.

61

62

63

62

Inside the vast and rather beautifully proportioned generator hall, three Siemens-Schuckert vertical-shaft alternator generators were originally installed. Each had a 30,000 kilowatt rating and were capable of delivering current at 10,500 volts into the transformer network. Only the top ends of these huge machines are seen in the photograph, the bulk of the generators being below the floor level. Further down again in the structure lay the three Francis-type turbines driven by the water from the canal, each giving around 30,000 horse-power at 150 revolutions per minute. Later, in 1934, a fourth turbo-alternator driven by a Kaplan turbine with a rating of 25,000 kilowatts was added to the system. This may seem small in terms of present-day output, but at the time there were criticisms of over-capacity. Such criticisms, however, were very soon proved groundless and this hydro-electric station became a real economic life-saver in the years ahead. Generation of electricity began in October 1929 and was in the hands of the Electricity Supply Board, a semi-state body established the previous year.

63

On 22 July 1929, with the canal, dam and powerhouse completed, water was first admitted to the system of the Shannon Scheme. The headrace was designed to furnish a flow of 500 cubic metres per second in the eight-mile-long canal.

64

On 9 September 1929, the most elaborate Civic Week Pageant yet to be held took place. It culminated in a dramatic performance at the Mansion House, Dublin, written and designed by Micheál mac Liammóir and produced by Hilton Edwards. Its conclusion was an apotheosis of the 1916 Rising, *Dublin 1916*, seen in this photograph during its revival a few months later at the Gate Theatre. *Tiny Tim*, the tallest member of the Dublin police, whose statuesque figure on point duty was well known to the public, played the part of a Formorian giant and the present writer's mother, who had been acting with the Gate since its inception, was assigned the part of Banba. In this role she had charge of two really enormous Irish wolfhounds, as distinct from the Irish deerhound which figures so prominently on the colophon of the Abbey Theatre. Despite their appearance, they were very gentle and friendly animals.

64

65

On 17 January 1930, this curtain parted to open a golden age of Dublin theatre, the like of which was not to be seen even to the present day. After an extensive and brilliant remodelling of the interior of the old building by a young architect, Michael Scott, the Gate Theatre opened its doors on an auditorium of 400 seats surrounded by rough-stippled dull gold walls and exciting jet black doorways and mouldings. Describing the stage facilities, Hilton Edwards said:

'It has not a cyclorama in the true meaning of the term, but a permanent, solid, curving sky behind which is a passage from one side of the stage to the other. At the base of the "sky" is a lighting pit five feet wide and four feet deep that can be covered at will and when uncovered can also be used as a lower stage level.'

Edwards described the lighting arrangements thus:

65

'Above and immediately behind the proscenium is a lighting bridge from which is suspended a battery of lanterns ... The lighting plant is simple but flexible and very efficient. It now (1935) consists of about twenty points wired to 500-watt dimmers and three points to 1,000-watt resistances. The overhead fore-stage lighting: one central 1,000-watt focus lantern and three 500-watt baby spots ... The lighting bridge equipment usually consists of one central 500-watt baby spot with on either side two 500-watt floods and two baby spots placed alternately. For use of the stage level are two tall and two short standards carrying a 500-watt flood and one standard carrying a 1,000-watt focus lantern that can be used on either side of the stage. The sky is lit above by one 1,000-watt horizon lantern and a batten of ten 100-candle-power blue lamps and from below in the pit by five 500-watt flood lanterns.'

If one compares this description of the resources of the Gate Theatre in the 1930s with the stage lighting of the Abbey today, one can fully appreciate the aesthetic genius and technical resourcefulness of Hilton Edwards and the part he played in bringing about a revolution in the dramatic use of light and colour on the Irish stage. The first production of the third season was Goethe's *Faust*.

66   67

66
Lennox Robinson, playwright, stage director and director of the Abbey Theatre Company Ltd. His first play was produced at the Abbey as early as 1908 and, from then on until the end of his life, he made a continuous contribution to the theatre as a playwright, producer and director of the company. In 1918, he founded the Dublin Drama League, with the support of W. B. Yeats. Both men believed that the tendency which the Abbey had shown under the influence of Synge and Lady Gregory, to confine its plays to the work of Irish playwrights, was debilitating and stultifying. They felt that important non-Irish drama should constantly form a part of the repertoire. The League, with its Saturday and Sunday performances at the Abbey, sought to remedy this and was the first to bring expressionist theatre to Dublin. As Robinson said: 'Here in Ireland we are isolated, cut off from the thought of the world ... I ask you, for the young

writer's sake, to open up the door and let us out of our prison.'

In 1921, when the Carnegie Trust became responsible for the establishment of free public libraries in Ireland, Lennox Robinson was appointed secretary and treasurer of the advisory committee which ran the service. But, in 1924, as a consequence of contributing a short story called 'The Madonna of Slieve Dun' to the literary magazine run by Francis Stuart, the committee was suspended and Robinson was removed from office, even though W. B. Yeats, then a Senator, had come to his defence in the strongest possible terms.

67
Even with an annual subsidy, the Abbey was having difficulty in maintaining its position. Age was beginning to tell on Lady Gregory and the meagre subsidy meant that the theatre was obliged to ensure full houses by putting on an increasing number of popular comedies. Important straight plays still formed part of the repertoire, including Brinsley McNamara's *The Master*, based on the mean, vindictive hostility his father had experienced after writing *The Valley of the Squinting Windows*. Yeats's interesting experiments in Japanese theatrical forms could not sustain a theatre the size of the Abbey, so with the loss of O'Casey, a more restricted repertoire characterised the output at this time.

68
Set for the first production of George Shiels's comedy *The New Gossoon* at the Abbey Theatre. Along with Lennox Robinson and Brinsley McNamara, George Shiels was a major contributor to the body of provincial town-and-country comedies that played such a large part in the Abbey Theatre repertoire at this time. A Belfastman, Shiels began his contribution to the Abbey seasons in 1921, but his best work was to come in the late twenties and early thirties.

68

69

The economic impact of the world depression which began with the Wall Street Crash of 1929 was making itself felt in Ireland. The cautious, ultra-conservative policies of Cumann na nGaedheal were beginning to meet increasing antipathy. Their one really bold innovation, the Shannon Scheme, had not begun to make much impact on country life as the process of rural electrification was not advanced widely enough for it to do so. In the spring, President Cosgrave opened a new area of wharfage at the port of Waterford.

69

70
The new wharf at Waterford, 1930. In spite of the bunting, unemployment at the ports and elsewhere in Ireland was rising, both south and north of the border. Discontent among the disenfranchised, left-wing Republicans was on the increase with more and more shootings and other violence, while Cosgrave's policy of suppression by means of the emergency powers was again filling the prisons.

70

71

At the Gate, *Faust* was succeeded by Balderston and Squire's *Berkeley Square*. A play with the theme of perceptual transferrence in time, it gave full scope to Edwards 's strong but sensitive direction and use of light to create atmosphere, with outstanding performances by mac Liammóir as Standish and Meriel Moore as Helen. neither Edwards nor mac Liammóir was really satisfied with the single setting, but their slender financial resources did not allow them to make it more elaborate or finished in appearance.

72

Florence Morrison as the Lady Anne Pettigrew in *Berkeley Square* at the Gate in March 1930. Later in the season, she was to play the part of Herloff's Marthe in *The Witch* by the Danish playwright Wiers Jensen. Many years later the play was made into the film *Vredens Dag* by Carl Theodor Dreyer.

73

After Fianna Fáil entered the Dáil in 1927, de Valera went to the United States to raise funds on behalf of the new political party. In November 1929, he again did this. But this time he had another very important project for which he also wanted to find financial help, the publishing of a new national newspaper. The national press at the time tended to support Cumann na nGaedheal and the new mass medium of radio was firmly under the control of the governing party. So, like others before him in a similar situation, de Valera was aware of the importance of establishing an organ of mass-communications on behalf of the Fianna Fáil party. Much of the support for this new venture came from Irish-American groups and individuals.

In May 1930, de Valera returned to Ireland to lay the groundwork for a serious electoral challenge to Cumann na nGaedheal as soon as the new newspaper was in full operation. It seems quite laughable to us today, but the Cumann na nGaedheal establishment of the time, as well as other even more right-wing groups, was continuously accusing both de Valera personally and the Fianna Fáil party in general of having Communist sympathies and preparing Red Revolution! Happily for our self respect, they did not press these absurdities to the length of treason trials in the McCarthy style. The American company, 'Irish Press Incorporated', held a controlling interest through Eamon de Valera himself, who was their representative on the Irish board.

74

After several dummy-runs, the first publication of the *Irish Press* took place on 5 September 1931. The editor was Frank Gallagher, though de Valera himself took close interest in both its content and style, working long hours in the newspaper office and supervising every detail of presentation. Publication had been achieved just in time, for only weeks later emergency powers as stringent as those during the Civil War were introduced by Cumann na nGaedheal, but the American ownership of the *Irish Press* would have made suppression of the paper difficult.

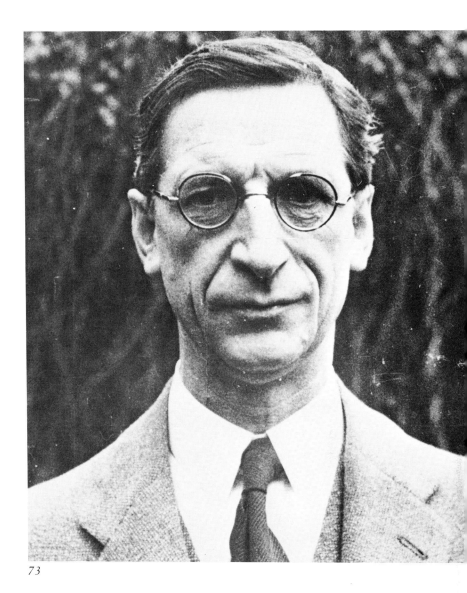

73

74

75

76

75

When President Cosgrave called for the dissolution of the Dáil in January and a general election in February 1932, things were very different from the situation that had existed in 1927. A world-wide depression had been biting for some years, and the Constitutional amendment, while giving satisfaction to the more authoritarian-minded supporters of Cumann na nGaedheal, had already spread a wide surge of alarm in other quarters. Some felt that a step had been taken over the threshold of military dictatorship and the overall control of the media of mass communication had been broken by the steadily growing influence of the *Irish Press*. Cosgrave had also been influenced in calling an early election because of the imminence of the Eucharistic Congress in June and the Imperial Conference in Canada in the following month. The summary convictions and jailings carried out by the Military Tribunal and the prosecution of the editor of the *Irish Press* under the Public Safety Act were a poor preparation for an electoral contest. To cap this, in a filmed interview a few days before polling day, Cosgrave had declared, 'Great Britain and Ireland are great emigrating countries — their sons, in a very real sense, inherit the Earth!' Hardly the right rallying cry for a community suffering from increasing unemployment.

76

De Valera speaking at Ennis, Co. Clare, February 1932.

77

In spite of wild charges of radical measures such as land confiscations which were intended to affect the farming vote, and the equally unfounded accusations of left-wing extremism which emanated from surprisingly sedate quarters, the authentic voice of what was in reality a very moderate, rather right of centre party, did get over to the electorate. Voters responded rather moderately too, giving no overall majority in the Dáil, but allowing Fianna Fáil to take power as a monority government with the support of the seven Labour Party TDs.

78

De Valera with his first cabinet, 9 March 1932. He had been elected to the presidency of the executive council on 9 March, by eighty-one votes to sixty-eight, with James Dillon and two other Independents voting for him as well as the Labour deputies. Within a matter of hours, the Minister for Justice and the Minister for Defence arrived at Arbour Hill Barracks where the majority of the ninety-seven political prisoners held under the powers of the Public Safety Act were confined. These prisoners included most of the leaders of the Socialist faction of the IRA, among them Charles and George Gilmore, Sean Hogan and Frank Ryan. Frank Aiken, having discovered the conditions under which the men were being held, ordered that these were to be improved at once and told the prisoners that they would all be released at the earliest possible moment.

77

78

79

The very next day, 10 March, the first twenty prisoners
were released from Arbour Hill, to receive an
enthusiastic greeting from a large crowd. Many of the
chief supporters of the Socialist left in Irish politics
were present. That indefatigable old fighter for the left
and for women's rights, Madame Despard, was there,
as was Madame Maud Gonne MacBride and her son
Sean MacBride. In the midst of the joyous crowd, one
great personality was missed, though remembered, one
who would most surely have been there had she been
alive: Madame Markievicz. Was there not to be a
possibility that a united Socialist left might be formed
to participate in constitutional politics?

80

President of the Executive Council, Eamon de Valera
and the Vice President, Sean T. O'Kelly, arrive at
number eleven Downing Street for the talks with the
British government on 9 June 1932. De Valera was
determined to implement Fianna Fáil's election
promises with as little delay as possible. The prisoners
had been released. Legislation to abolish the oath of
allegiance to the crown, though being delayed by the
Senate, was in progress.

But a most serious sticking point also in negotiation
with the British was over the changes proposed to the
'ultimate financial agreement' of 1925. In that year,
while on the run, the Socialist Republican Peadar
O'Donnell had started a campaign in the poorer parts
of the west of Ireland to encourage people to refuse to
pay the land annuities which under the agreement
finalised by Ernest Blythe, were being remitted to the
British treasury. Fianna Fáil had taken this up as an
extremely important plank in their election campaign.
They felt it would benefit the small farmer, though the
big 'beef barons' who exported cattle on the hoof to
England would feel the first effects of any British
reprisals.

79   80

81
Back in Dublin, the biggest public event ever to take place in Ireland was under way, the Eucharistic Congress. The architect J. J. Robinson was commissioned to design the temporary buildings that were to furnish the settings for the ceremonies, such as this altar pavilion on O'Connell Bridge, Dublin.

82
The largest structure was the pavilion and colonnade in the Phoenix Park. Looking back with the dispassionate eye of distance, one is struck by the impression that the architectural effect is more reminiscent of British India than of Bernini.

83
Over a million people attended mass in the Phoenix Park, a scene that was not to be repeated until the visit of Pope John Paul II in 1979.

83

82

84

The town of Carlow, from the air. With the ending of the Eucharistic Congress, people's attention became focused on the changes that had come about due to the withholding of the Land Annuity payments to the United Kingdom. As a result, the British government was now imposing a punitive taxation on Irish goods of many kinds. This fell most heavily on the large farmers, beef producers and cattle exporters, those groups which had been, in the main, supporters of Cumann na nGaedheal. Though most unpopular in that sector of the agricultural electorate, the small farmers, particularly those at the level of subsistence farming in the south, west and Donegal, had voted for just such a policy in the election and had been a factor in the rise of the Fianna Fáil poll. It was also Fianna Fáil policy that the previous government's efforts to increase the country's self-sufficiency in electric power and in sugar beet production and processing should be extended to many other areas. They were particularly eager that the country's economic dependence on the live meat trade should be modified by a large increase in tillage, especially for the production of wheat, thus making it possible to achieve something approaching self-sufficiency in basic foods.

85

Domhnall Ó Buachalla, in the garden of his house. During the summer of 1932, relations between the Fianna Fáil administration and the Governor-General, James MacNeill, became ever more strained. In September, the Irish government formally asked for his removal from office, nominating in his stead Domhnall Ó Buachalla, a 1916 veteran from Maynooth, prominent in the Irish language revival movement and a loyal supporter of Fianna Fáil from its inception.

86

The last Governor-General of the Irish Free State reads his letter of appointment to office in November 1932.

84

Faithful to the trust placed in him by de Valera, Ó Buachalla took no part in any public ceremonial or function. He did not reside in the Vice-Regal Lodge but lived in a modest Dublin house and engaged solely in private activities but for the occasional act of giving his signature to certain acts of the Oireachtas and to the instrument ordering the dissolution of the Dáil. This reduced the status of the king's representative in the Free State to a ghostly condition for the few years that remained until the office was abolished under the provisions of the Statute of Westminster, which the previous administration, particularly in the person of Patrick McGilligan had done so much to bring about,

85   *86*

87

De Valera arrives, in the midst of a welcoming crowd of supporters, to open the Fianna Fáil campaign in the general election of January 1933. At the end of the previous year he had decided that being kept in office by the grace of the Labour Party and a very small number of Independents was too insecure a basis for the legislative programme which would be needed to deal with the problems of the 'economic war' with the United Kingdom and the other pressing problems of the 1930s. He announced the dissolution of the Dáil on 2 January 1933.

87

88

88
De Valera speaking at Ennis, January 1933. He feared
the pressure that might be exerted by Westminster on
Cumann na nGaedheal and the National Centre Party,
formed in September 1932 to represent farming
interests. He was determined to increase Fianna Fáil's
representation by a programme of protection for Irish
industries, the retention of the Land Annuity funds
and their reduction by half.

89

A Cumann na nGaedheal election meeting in Dublin, January 1933. As the last general election had shown, the normal processes of elective democracy in a country which had relatively recently had a civil war are necessarily fraught with considerable tension, in contrast to countries with a more placid political history. Republican sympathisers had not felt it possible to participate in parliamentary democracy due to the oath and a refusal to concede legitimacy to the Cumann na nGaedheal administrations. They had suffered deprivation and imprisonment, and now they frequently resorted to violent disruptive assaults during Cumann na nGaedheal election meetings. The situation was aggravated, however, by the politicising of the Army Comrades Association, a body which had begun with the apparent intention of being merely a benevolent group. It had been formed less than a year before, on 9 February 1932, largely on the initiative of Commandant Edward Cronin. Drawing its membership from both serving and retired members of the Free State Army, it inevitably had an anti-Republican and anti-Fianna Fáil bias which was greatly increased in the summer of 1932 when a number of prominent Cumann na nGaedheal figures, such as Ernest Blythe, Dr T. F. O'Higgins and General Mulcahy became associated with its leadership. Although it claimed to be non-political and willing to protect freedom of speech at any political meeting, there was no way in which a body with such a history and such a leadership could really expect the confidence and co-operation of Fianna Fáil and the Republicans, and the presence of ACA members at meetings, marching and acting as stewards led to further polarisation and violence.

90

Civic Guards keeping order while W. T. Cosgrave, leader of Cumann na nGaedheal, addresses the meeting in Dublin, January 1933. It was de Valera's contention, and the policy of Fianna Fáil, that only one body of men was appropriate for keeping order during political meetings — the police.

91

In his appeal to the electorate, W. T. Cosgrave promised an end to the tariff war with the United Kingdom 'in three days', to suspend payments of the Land Annuities to London for two years and to reduce all the Land Annuities by half. As well as this, the Cumann na nGaedheal campaign had been characterised by accusations that de Valera and Fianna Fáil were in the hands of 'red revolutionaries' who were only waiting for de Valera to be returned to power to overturn constitutional government. Ireland is, on the whole, unfavourable ground for public smear campaigns of this kind, being a small country where there is a largely homogeneous social structure with a wide range of personal intercommunication. The election results were to show that the campaign had been a complete failure. As for the overturning of a constitutional party-political system, it was soon to be seen that such a threat would come not from the left, but from the right.

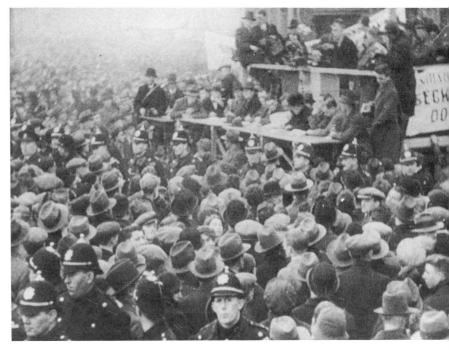

89

90

91

92

93

92
Cumann na nGaedheal election posters, January 1933.

93
Fianna Fáil election poster. The plainer, matter of fact style makes an interesting contrast with the 'razmataz' of the opposition.

94

95

96

94
On polling day, a poor Dublin mother brings her family with her while she records her vote. The wearing of shawls by working-class women in Dublin continued until some years after the Second World War.

95
The Lord Mayor of Dublin, 'Alfie' Byrne, arrives to cast his vote. A conservatively orientated Independent TD, he consistently supported Cumann na nGaedheal and, later, Fine Gael. But on account of accessibility to his constituents and the readiness with which he took up individual cases of hardship, he was perhaps the most popular Lord Mayor of Dublin this century.

96
Mr and Mrs W. T. Cosgrave, after having recorded their votes, 1933.

97

Fianna Fáil was returned with the first overall majority in
the history of the state, with seventy-seven seats,
Cumann na nGaedheal dropping to forty-eight, and
Labour gaining one to give eight. The new Centre
Party, formed from an absorption of the National
League, the Farmers and some Independents, returned
eleven, while the Independents, mainly through losses
to the Centre Party, sank to nine. Here de Valera
makes a speech in which he says that Fianna Fáil can
now look forward to applying the policies that will
increase national self-sufficiency.

98

'Alfie' Byrne, re-elected as an Independent, gives thanks
to his Dublin constituents.

97

99

De Valera with the Executive Council, 1933. There were some minor changes from the cabinet of 1932. P. J. Rutledge replaced James Geoghegan as Minister for Justice. Rutledge had been Minister for Lands and Fisheries where his place was now taken by Senator Joseph Connolly, while Gerald Boland was appointed Minister for Posts and Telegraphs. With a clear majority, all seemed set for a rapid implementation of the plans that had been in preparation, but the future is always surprising, and events were to force the government away from the path of political liberalisation and peaceful development that had been envisaged.

100

General Eoin O'Duffy, who had had a successful career in the Free State Army both during and after the Civil War, was Commissioner of Police during the ten years of the Cumann na nGaedheal administration and during the Fianna Fáil minority government. Disruption of political meetings had increased further and clashes between IRA supporters and the increasingly militant Army Comrades Association had become an ever more serious problem. It was de Valera's policy that only one body should have the task of keeping order at public meetings: the police. As he had shown on coming to power in 1932, he also believed in the continuity of the civil service in a democratic state. It was with great reluctance therefore that, notwithstanding O'Duffy's very able handling of the arrangements for the Eucharistic Congress, de Valera came to believe that he would be obliged to ask O'Duffy to take another position of equal status in the permanent Civil Service. This the Commissioner refused to do, and on 22 February 1933, he was dismissed. The Chief of the Detective Division, Colonel Eamon Broy, was appointed in his place. Though Republicans were pleased at this change, it caused great — though as it turned out unjustified — disquiet among supporters of Cumann na nGaedheal and a vitriolic debate in the Dáil resulted, in which a number of opposition deputies took part. The leader of the opposition, W. T. Cosgrave, claimed that Fianna Fáil had been pressurised into the decision by 'Communist-IRA extremists'. But in the light of subsequent events, it would be truer to say that the Fianna Fáil cabinet were alarmed by undercurrents in the ACA which manifested some characteristics of Italian Fascism. They feared an attempt at a corporatist *putsch*. Five months later, after continual pressure from the more right wing elements in Cumann na nGaedheal, notably Ernest Blythe and Professor Michael Tierney of UCD, O'Duffy accepted the nomination for leadership of the ACA, being elected to that position on 20 July. Immediately he announced far-reaching changes in the organisation. Its name was changed to the 'National Guard'; it adopted a corporatist political programme and a religious test was applied to all seeking membership. The wearing of uniforms was continued. In view of such developments, the unease of the Fianna Fáil cabinet in earlier months in relation to the ACA becomes understandable.

98

99
100

A Blueshirt parade, Carrick-on-Suir, Co. Tipperary,
July 1933. Within a week of becoming leader of the
reconstituted ACA, now open to a wider membership
and becoming a frankly right-wing political body,
O'Duffy claimed that its membership exceeded thirty
thousand and parades and marches became daily more
frequent. O'Duffy announced that there would be
participation from all over the country in a giant
commemorative march to Leinster Lawn in Dublin, in
which he expected twenty thousand National Guard to
take part.

101

Only eleven days after the banning of the National Guard, a most astonishing event took place among the Irish opposition parties of the right. Cumann na nGaedheal and the Centre Party merged, drawing into their net as they did so some of the Independents. More remarkable still, however, was that the new party also incorporated the National Guard as an autonomous body within its structure. W. T. Cosgrave even stepped down to hand the leadership of the new party, to be known as the United Ireland Party — Fine Gael, over to General O'Duffy! Cosgrave, however, kept for himself the leadership of Fine Gael in the Dáil. Although Sean Lemass satirically referred to the new party as the 'Cripple Alliance', it was to prove a very dangerous threat to open democratic development in Ireland, having declared corporatist intentions and almost at once relaunching the National Guard under a new name — the Young Ireland Association.

Using the reactivated Constitutional Amendment No. 17 and the reconstituted military tribunal, and in furtherance of the policy that there should be only one army and one police force, de Valera now began to arrest, try and intern both Blueshirts and members of the IRA, where there was evidence that they had excercised those functions. As a further move against the Blueshirts, he made a determined effort to prohibit the wearing of uniforms. The police were encouraged to arrest those wearing them. To strengthen the government's hand in this, the Wearing of Uniforms (Restriction) Bill was passed through the Dáil, after vituperative debate, on 14 March 1934. Almost immediately this Bill was rejected by the Senate and could not come into force for a further eighteen months, despite its second passage through the Dáil. Police pressure against the wearing of the Blueshirt uniform was kept up. Here a body of Blueshirts are seen concealing their uniforms under their overcoats until they have formed up to march.

Meanwhile, the Fianna Fáil administration was becoming increasingly worried that a right-wing *putsch* was in preparation and made vigorous efforts to call in all the arms held by members of the National Guard who had kept their hand guns after retiring from the Free State Army. Indeed, a report submitted to Geoghegan by O'Duffy when he was Commissioner of Police in September 1932 stated of the then ACA:

'The organisation has the support of members of the late government, the most active being General Mulcahy. Mr Blythe supports the organisation through the medium of the *United Irishman*. The majority of Cumann na nGaedheal TDs and ex-army officers throughout the Saorstát are also organising. There is no doubt that a considerable number of ex-army officers are in possession of revolvers, and even rifles, held surreptitiously, as souvenirs of the pre-Truce period. Further, many ex-National Army men, when leaving the army in 1923-25 brought arms with them. Should the movement at any time desire to adopt other than constitutional methods, it can, without doubt, lay hands on a sufficient quantity of arms and ammunition to render it a very formidable insurrectionary force, and a source of extreme danger to the peace and stability of the country.'

Fianna Fáil did not take this threat lightly. As the date of the march drew near, large numbers of police were brought into Government Buildings, and beds and bedding with them. The police throughout the country were placed on alert and many were drafted into the capital. O'Duffy called off the march on Dublin but ordered the National Guard to hold marches on 20 August, throughout the country. On 21 August, the government ironically made use of a reactivation of Constitutional Amendment No. 17, introduced in 1931 by Cumann na nGaedheal, proclaiming the National Guard illegal and reconstituting the military tribunal.

104

Newtownbarry Fair, Co. Wexford. By the spring of
1934, the escalating tariff war between the United
Kingdom and the Free State had brought about a crisis
of the first magnitude in the cattle trade. Nine-tenths
of the export market from the cattle raising counties
— Carlow, Cork, Kildare, Kilkenny, Limerick, Meath,
Tipperary, Waterford, Westmeath and Wexford — had
gone to the English market. Now the accumulation of
unsold beasts brought about a singularly inept piece of
legislation in the form of the Calf Slaughter Scheme,
introduced by the Minister for Agriculture, Dr James
Ryan. The effect of this was most keenly felt by
farmers with large and middle-sized holdings who
began to protest by witholding the payment of rates.
This was an issue quickly exploited by O'Duffy as
leader of Fine Gael and the Blueshirts. When bailiffs
were sent in to seize cattle and other assets, and when
auctions of these goods were held, disruptive action
and protest marches were organised in which the
Blueshirts figured prominently. The local government

104

elections were approaching, which, ironically in the context, were to be held for the last time, not under universal, but under 'rated occupier' franchise. Since this favoured landed proprietors, Fine Gael assumed it would produce an overwhelming vote in their favour. As things turned out, the very reverse was the case and Fianna Fáil came out the winner, gaining one hundred and thirty-two more council seats than Fine Gael.

107

105

On 8 December 1933, the Blueshirts were once more banned under their new name of the Young Ireland Association. Six days later they appeared again, exactly as before, but now calling themselves the League of Youth. The structure of the organisation was becoming increasingly authoritarian and tending more and more towards Fascist models. Opposition from Fianna Fáil and IRA sympathisers increased, so that sometimes the police were unable to keep order and the military had to be called out. After the failure of Fine Gael in the local elections, the speeches of the Blueshirt leaders began to take on a more menacing tone. Commandant Cronin said at a meeting in Tipperary: 'De Valera has spoken about a dictatorship, but I say here tonight if a dictatorship is necessary for the Irish people we are going to have one.' While in Limerick, Captain Quish exclaimed: 'The government are a crowd of Spaniards, Jews and Manxmen. If necessary we will use the guns again to redeem the people.'

106

General O'Duffy takes the salute from a crowd of Blueshirts in the garden of the Mansion House, Dublin, 19 August 1934. The Congress of the League of Youth was attended by over a thousand delegates and the main resolution, which called for direct action in the rates strike by the illegal withholding of Land Annuity payments, was proposed by O'Duffy and passed with that unanimity which is so much the style of totalitarian gatherings. There was but one dissenting voice, that of Dr T. P. O'Higgins, who had sought to have the motion withdrawn.

107

General O'Duffy speaks at a Blueshirt meeting, 1934. The increasingly irredentist tone of his speeches and his repeated assertions that party politics should give way to a vocationally elected chamber, with the implication that the League of Youth be left as the one remaining political organism in a one-party state, so alarmed the party politicians in Fine Gael that he was prevailed upon to resign. He claimed that he had not resigned as head of the Blueshirts but, with the backing of Fine Gael, Commandant Edmund Cronin took over the leadership of the League of Youth and that body soon split into a Cronin and an O'Duffy faction. O'Duffy's last political act of consequence was to lead some seven hundred volunteers to fight under General Franco in the Spanish Civil War.

105

106

108

Michael Dolan and Eileen Crowe in the comedy by George Shiels, *Grogan and the Ferret* at the Abbey Theatre, 13 November 1933. Lady Gregory had died in 1932 and, the following year, with the crisis of the 'economic war' on their hands, the Fianna Fáil administration felt obliged to reduce the Abbey subsidy to £750 per annum. The great depression and the cut in the subsidy compelled the theatre to undertake American tours. The first, in 1931, was completed without incident. But in the following year, they were viciously attacked in New York when the United Irish-American Societies passed a resolution calling upon the Irish government to remove the subsidy altogether, as the performance of Synge's *Playboy of the Western World* and O'Casey's *The Plough and the Stars* gave a wrong impression of Irish life and character! It is

typical of de Valera that, after a discussion with W. B. Yeats, he refused to do this although the economic circumstances would have given the administration a ready excuse. The Irish government confined itself to having a note put on the programme saying that it did not have responsibility for the selection of plays for performance. The Abbey maintained its performances at home with the younger players, while the principal company was on tour. It had not yet begun to respond to the challenge of the new, permanent, alternative theatre in Dublin.

109

Ernest Blythe had been elected to the Senate in 1934. He and Professor Michael Tierney of UCD had been the principal ideologues behind the policy of the Blueshirts movement and had been responsible for much of the content of O'Duffy's speeches, for the General was an athlete rather than an intellectual. However, in the end, their creation got out of hand and frightened the party politicians of Fine Gael. Blythe and Tierney were obliged to retire from active political life, the latter going to UCD where he was eventually to become President; the former into the Abbey Theatre, first, in 1935, as a Director of the Board and later, Managing Director and owner of the majority of the private share capital of the National Theatre Society Ltd.

109

110

Set for *You Never Can Tell* by George Bernard Shaw at the Abbey Theatre, 26 December 1933. Although showing a greater degree of care than characterised by sets of the twenties, it is still visually unimaginative in concept, scenery, lighting and set-dressing. The general level of visual presentation was far behind that found at the Gate Theatre at the same time. With a view to catching up, the following year the theatre board brought in an English producer, Bladon Peake, together with the designer James Bould. They did a short season of European plays, Bould dispensing with the front curtain and building an apron stage. Unhappily, at that very disturbed time, when violent meetings and marches were taking place, the season was a financial failure and the directors decided to close the theatre down in January 1935 and prepare plans for a complete reorganisation of both the administration and the direction.

110

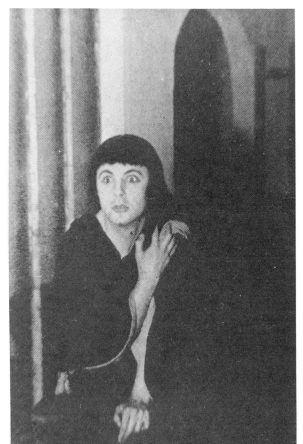

112

111

The Old Lady Says No at the Gate Theatre, 3 February 1931. The imaginative set design, stagecraft and lighting at the Gate had opened the eyes of Dubliners to a new dimension of theatre. The unique complementary talents and personalities of the principals and the gifted cast which supported them gave a style and *élan* to their work which was enormously stimulating. In the initial stages they also had an advantage over the Abbey, with only a very small number of directors on the board of the Dublin Gate Theatre Company Ltd. In the beginning there were only four: Hilton Edwards, Micheál mac Liammóir, 'Toto' Cogley and Gearoid O'Lochlainn. Policy making decisions were more easily reached and, as all were enthusiastic about transforming the character of theatre in Dublin, there were no contending factions. The photograph shows the extraordinarily intense atmosphere achieved by grouping and lighting alone and the strange, compelling effect of the apparently elongated, pointing arms, brought about by clever grouping and playing, a far cry from the 'literary theatre'.

112

Micheál mac Liammóir as Clarence in Shakespeare's *Richard III*. An actor of extraordinary versatility, power and visual awareness, he contrived to give himself a perfect period face in the part. This was the first production of *Richard III* by the Dublin Gate Theatre and it opened on 24 October 1933.

111

113

113

Ferenc Molnar's *Liliom*, which opened on 13 February, 1934, was notable for an exceptionally imaginative use of visual atmosphere, created by establishing miniature sets and a few salient objects with brilliantly emotive lighting. Writing a few months later Hilton Edwards said:

> 'In *Liliom* this was developed by the addition of an absolutely negative surrounding blackness, in the midst of which each set was created either by screens for interiors, or by objects for exteriors, e.g., there was a tree, a seat, a lighted lamp-post and some railings. For the railway embankment, telegraph poles and the railway track sloped in the suggestion of foreshortened perspective.'

This technique was carried even further in Edwards's production of Lord Longford's adaptation of Sheridan Le Fanu's story *Carmilla*. Edward Longford had bought the seven hundred unsold shares of the Dublin Gate Theatre Co. Ltd in 1931.

114

The Great Bolshevik Bugaboo proved to be as unreal an assessment as such opportunist black propaganda usually is. By 1935, the old establishment had found that de Valera was, so far as the Irish political spectrum was concerned, very much a middle-of-the-road politician who was not about to overturn the state with a Red Army of Republicans. It is interesting to speculate what were the interests that lay behind the widespread campaign, though hard to run them definitively to earth. Certainly, Whitehall would have preferred to see the Cosgrave administration still in

114

the saddle. The photograph shows de Valera at the
Royal Dublin Society on the opening day of the Horse
Show, 1935.

115
De Valera was determined to have only one army. The
Blueshirt movement having been broken, he
consolidated his position by bringing the militant
factions of the IRA under increasing pressure, using
the legislation introduced by Cumann na nGaedheal to
do so. Here he takes the salute at a review of the
National Army. The change of regime had led to a
change in helmets for the troops, from that of the
British Army to that of the Wehrmacht.

115

116
On horseback, in 'Anthony Eden' hat and cloak, de Valera reviews the Air Corps. The aircraft, which differ little in general configuration from the one which Michael Collins bought in 1921, were replaced three years later by Gloster Gladiators.

117
De Valera, accompanied by his bodyguard, on his way to the eye clinic in Zurich, 25 March 1936. Malcolm MacDonald had replaced J. H. Thomas as the Dominions Secretary at Whitehall. MacDonald was convinced that an initiative from London might begin to resolve the numerous outstanding problems with the Irish Free State. So through the good offices of the Irish High Commissioner in London, John Dulanty, a secret meeting was arranged with de Valera at the Grosvenor Hotel, Victoria Station, as he was returning from this visit to Switzerland. This meeting led to further exploratory talks, which led in their turn to further direct meetings between de Valera and MacDonald in 1937.

117

116

Curtain designed by Micheál mac Liammóir for the 1936 production of *Twelfth Night* at the Gate Theatre. The exciting sets and graphic design at the Gate, as well as the forceful production techniques, had persuaded the board of the Abbey Theatre, in 1935, to invite the English producer Hugh Hunt to come over and work with them. He brought with him a young designer of sensitivity and talent, Tanya Moïsewitch, whose work was to open up perspectives beyond the symmetrical, rectilinear, 'fourth wall' box-set that had been such a predominating style for interiors at that theatre.

119
The Earl of Longford, Edward Pakenham. In his autobiography, *All for Hecuba*, Micheál mac Liammóir, quoting Hilton Edwards, writes:

> 'Here we're drifting along with Edward Longford taking the reins, a rich man new to the theatre, forcing the pace with plays that are just wrong, paying salaries to an increasing number of amateurs, lending us money whenever we get into a hole. And apart from Edward it's hopeless: the Gate would be dead without him probably. I tell you there aren't enough people.'

Without financial assistance it was sadly apparent that Dublin could not support permanent theatre. It was also clear that the stresses inside the Gate were reaching a crisis which culminated in 1936. While the Gate was on tour in Egypt, Lord Longford brought a second company to London under the name of the Dublin Gate Theatre. After this, a split was inevitable. It was arranged that the two companies should share the Gate Theatre on a six-months-each basis, mac Liammóir-Edwards Productions for six months, Longford Productions for six months. But the schism was not without great bitterness at the time, for many who admired the unique creativity of mac Liammóir and Edwards felt that they had been betrayed. The acerbity of this feeling is to be found in an epigram which circulated in Dublin:

118

119

121

'Fair, fat and orchidectomised, pink, perspiring and profuse.
My Lord, your eighty-thousand income lends the illusion that you've got a use!'

120

The graphic artist, composer and actor Art O'Murnaghan was another of the very talented people who contributed so much to the Gate Theatre. A gentle, strong and kind man, wise and original in thought, he contributed richly from his many gifts to the magic that was the Gate Theatre in the thirties. As well as designing, composing music and acting, he was a stage manager of genius. The present writer recalls his many kindnesses to a child of seven years, and again to a young man of twenty. His great life's work was the *Leabhar na hAiséirghe*, an incredibly beautiful series of the most exquisite illuminations on vellum which he began in 1924 and completed in 1951, three years before his death. As well as all this, O'Murnaghan was a teacher of art and a prominent member of the Votaries of Aengus.

121

Liam O'Leary, from Youghal in Co. Cork, was, with Edward Toner, the founder of the Irish Film Society in 1936. In the days of severe censorship the institution of a Film Society was a paramount necessity. They made a beginning with the showing of Sergei Eisenstein's *Potemkin*, and were astounded to find their activities vilified in newspapers of a certain class in the following terms:

SPREADING DEATHLY POISON
FIRST SOVIET PROPAGANDA FILM IN IRELAND
SUBTLE SUBVERSIVE MANOEUVRES EXPOSED
A CALL FOR GOVERNMENT ACTION

Being sane, sensible and strong-minded individuals, O'Leary and Toner stuck it out and the Irish Film Society went from strength to strength to become an institution of real cultural value over many years. O'Leary went on to become an actor, producer-director and Ireland's leading film archivist and author of books on cinema.

120

On 27 May 1936, an airline calling itself Irish Sea Airways began operations by opening a passenger service between Dublin and Bristol. It was the first Irish airline and it was to become Aer Lingus. Dublin Airport had not yet come into existence and the service was operated from Baldonnel, the military airfield in south Co. Dublin, where the first aircraft, a De Havilland 'Dragon' is standing in front of the hangar. The *Iolar* (Eagle) could accommodate five passengers as well as the pilot and co-pilot, but luggage was necessarily much restricted. The normal cruising speed of the *Iolar* was 132 mph at two thousand feet. A second similar aircraft was soon acquired and the services were extended to the Isle of Man, Liverpool and London by the end of the year. The *Iolar* was sold in 1938 and left Ireland to work on the service between St Just airfield, near Land's End, and St

Mary's in the Isles of Scilly. In 1941, while operating that service on behalf of her new owners, she was shot down into the sea by a German warplane. The De Havilland 'Dragons' were replaced by a Douglas DC3, bought in California, flown across the United States, taken apart, shipped to Antwerp, re-assembled and flown from a military airfield in Belgium to Ireland just a fortnight before the German invasion. It was this later type, the versatile DC3, with which Aer Lingus maintained a service between Dublin and Liverpool throughout the war. After the war's cessation in Europe, Aer lingus began flying to Northolt, near London, and began building up its post-war route network before the introduction of the turbo-prop aircraft. During the war-time service, the windows of the DC3 were fitted with translucent covering which let in light but prevented the passengers from seeing out.

123

On 1 May 1937, de Valera published the draft of a new Constitution, which contained no mention of the crown as the head of the British Commonwealth of Nations but did contain provisions that were regarded by some as reactionary and sectarian. George Bernard Shaw, always a keen observer of Irish political developments, noticed that the document was retrogressive in its attitude to women's status, with which view quite a number of women in Ireland today would agree. He also believed that the innovation of the office of President of Ireland would give the holder dictatorial powers, a prediction that has, of course, proved wholly inaccurate. The constitutional draft was approved by the Dáil in June, with surprisingly little opposition to its major provisions from Fine Gael. Before it was put to a plebiscite, simultaneously with a general election, de Valera called upon all the Irish judges to swear to uphold it, making it clear to them that any who did not do so would be regarded as having resigned from the bench. It seems most remarkable that the constitutionality of this singular excercise of *force majeure* was not tested at the time. The plebiscite produced a 13 per cent majority in favour of the Constitution and it came into force on 29 December 1937. There is today a growing opposition to a number of its aspects, both in regard to the position of women in late twentieth-century society and to the question of the ban on divorce, which many now regard as being inimical to the reunification of Ireland.

123

124

124
The Taoiseach, Eamon de Valera and, at left, Dr James Ryan, the Minister for Agriculture, on their way to Downing Street. The Irish delegation also consisted of Sean MacEntee, Minister for Finance and Sean Lemass, Minister for Industry and Commerce. They arrived in London on 16 January 1938 to begin on the following day the conference that was fundamentally to alter the relationship between the United Kingdom and what had been the Irish Free State, soon officially to be called Éire. The conference brought to an end the tariff 'war', resulted in the return of the British occupied ports and enabled Éire to remain neutral in the Second World War.

125

125
Dr Douglas Hyde, the Gaelic scholar and writer (An Craoibhín Aoibhinn) and co-founder with Eoin Mac Neill of the Gaelic League, became the first President of Éire under the new constitution. Here he arrives to take up residence in Áras an Uachtaráin, formerly the vice-Regal Lodge, on 4 May 1938.

126
De Valera inspects the Guard of Honour of the Irish Army garrison of Spike Island, 17 June 1938.

127
According to the terms of the new accord reached with Whitehall, the last British troops left the twenty-six counties on 17 June 1938. Here they are seen leaving Spike Island, in Cork Harbour.

128
June 1938 saw another general election, in which the Fianna Fáil administration consolidated its position, winning seventy-seven seats, which left de Valera with a clear majority of sixteen seats over the combined opposition. It was just as well that the political situation had defined itself in this way, as the Munich crisis was building to its climax.

126

127

128

129

The Control Room, Ardnacrusha. A fourth hydro-turbo-alternator, using a Kaplan turbine, had been added to the generating station in 1934. It was to prove invaluable in the years immediately ahead. Total output of Ardnacrusha was now eighty-five megawatts.

130

The main features of the distribution grid of 110,000 volts were now in operation, carried by pylons of German design like these near Newbridge, Co. Kildare.

131

Step-down transformer being installed at Portlaw, Co. Waterford, 1938. An essential step in the actual use of the power at local level and in the rural electrification scheme, the coming war was to hamper the development for many years.

129

131

130

Gaeltarra Éireann workshop, Belmullet, Co. Mayo. Set up to assist the continuation of spoken Irish in those remote areas where the language had survived, these workshops provided employment, helped offset the effects of emigration and produced woollen goods and toys for export. It will be seen that electric light had reached this remote town by July 1958.

132

135

133

Although electricity had reached small towns in the remotest part of Co. Mayo, conditions for bringing children to school in that notoriously wet region were of the most primitive, if they existed at all. Here, in June 1938, Crossmolina children are boarding the horse-drawn school van, a vehicle almost completely without windows and of an austere character more suitable for the members of a rigidly enclosed order than for young children, though one has to observe that the two barefooted boys must have been very glad of it.

134

1938 also saw a very important event in the history of communications, the inauguration of the scheduled flying-boat service across the North Atlantic. In 1936, Germany had initiated a scheduled passenger air service across the North Atlantic, from Frankfurt am Main to New York by means of the hydrogen-filled rigid airship *Hindenberg* which could make the journey

in just under three days. This service came to an end with the *Hindenberg* disaster at Lakehurst, New Jersey, in 1937; as it was coming in to land, the hydrogen caught fire and the great airship, the largest ever built, crashed several hundred feet to the ground in a mass of flames. In the mid-thirties, largely due to its unhappy experience with the airship R101, the British government had decided to improve the postal air services throughout the Commonwealth by replacing the great biplanes that had operated a passenger and mail service through the Imperial Airways company by large flying-boats. Built by Shortts, these revolutionary aircraft, the 'Empire' Flying-boats, proved exceptionally efficient and reliable and their crews became accustomed to making long flights over water and desert. Imperial Airways decided that the collapse of the German scheduled service would facilitate the launching of their North Atlantic service, which they had long been planning. In the event, they decided to operate it jointly with the most important of the American long-distance air carriers, Pan-American. Here Imperial Airways' flying boat *Cambria* taxis away from the vicinity of Foynes pier, Co. Limerick, to take off from the smooth waters of the Shannon on the first flight. Simultaneously, a Pan-American flying boat was preparing to leave the United States.

135

De Valera stands on Foynes pier, watching for the first Pan-American 'Clipper' to arrive in Ireland, in order to welcome and congratulate the crew.

134

136

The Pan-American 'Clipper' arriving at Foynes. Like the 'Empire' Flying-boats, these early forms of flying-boats used by Pan-American had wing-tip floats to stabilise the water-tight hull. It appears considerably smaller and more primitive than the British flying-boat, but Pan-American had built up a considerable experience of long, over-water flights in the service from the US to Hawaii. Later versions of the Pan-American 'Clippers' were to dispense with the wing-tip floats and make use instead of sponsons, a form of thick, hollow, stub-wings which gave extra flotation and stability to the hull, emerging from it approximately where the lower part of the struts do in this earlier form of the 'Clipper'. Sponsons had the additional advantage of making a convenient platform from which passengers could step into a motorboat.

136

137

On the way from Galway to the Aran Islands, 6 August 1938, on board the SS *Dun Aengus*. This remarkable old vessel, built by the Dublin Dockyard Company Ltd and launched in 1912, operated a steamship service to the Aran Islands for the Galway Bay Steamboat Company from that year until it was taken over by CIE in 1951. She continued in service until she was replaced in 1958 by the Diesel motor-vessel, *Naomh Éanna*, also built by the Dublin Dockyard Co. Ltd. She had a simple type of marine compound engine with just a high-pressure and a low-pressure cylinder, but the low freeboard of her well-deck enabled cattle and goods to be easily handled over the side when standing off Inishmaan and Inisheer. At Inishmore, she came alongside the pier to discharge her passengers and cargo. So reliable was she that, when she came under the ownership of CIE, she was the oldest railway-owned passenger vessel in Western Europe.

137

138

In a scene that has hardly changed in character from the 1930s until today, Aran Islanders at Kilronan wait outside the post office for the mail to arrive from the boat. Nowadays there would be fewer shawls in evidence, unless worn by tourists.

139

A weaver at work in his shed, Inishmore. The painted decorations on the frame of the loom are interesting.

140

A cottage interior, Inishmore. The clothes, drying in the cavernous fireplace remind one of the incessant damp. The pattern-printed oilcloth on the table is now as much a period curiosity as the three-legged pot, on the fireplace crane, in which a meal is cooking. The resigned body-mechanic of the two women is particularly telling as well as the daughter's figure, with cropped hair and steel-rimmed glasses, darning stockings in poor light. All presents a very different atmosphere from the romantic image sentimentally adhered to by some Irish writers of the earlier years of the twentieth century.

138

139

140

141

Then as now, the Aran Islands had an all-year-round tourist season and the fascination of watching curraghs manoeuvring on the surface of the open Atlantic can be enjoyed from the high cliffs. Nor have tourists changed in thier admiration for the Aran *crios* such as the girl on the right has bought.

142

Harvesting oats with sickles by Iron Age technology at Oatquarter, Inishmore. This particular small, level area on Inishmore has a thicker cover of soil and better drainage than anywhere else on the islands and is virtually the only place where any quantity of cereal crops can be raised. On the skyline on the right is the great, semi-circular Iron Age fort of Dun Aengus, beyond which the cliffs drop a sheer three hundred feet into the sea.

141

142

143
Poor conditions were not confined to the west of Ireland. Here on the platform of Fethard Station, Co. Waterford, in September 1938, two barefooted boys who should be at school are at work — for whom?

143

144

In the mid 1930s, the board of the Abbey Theatre was enlarged to include Ernest Blythe, Fred Higgins and Brinsley McNamara, who had been the author of that excellent study of Irish Grundyism, *The Valley of the Squinting Windows*, an achievement for which he would not only feel the heavy hand of censorship, but also be molested in his profession of teacher. Yeats remained on the board, but was now aging rapidly. Nonetheless, he had been largely instrumental in having the Abbey produce Sean O'Casey's *The Silver Tassie*, with sets by Maurice McGonigal.

Once again an outcry from certain quarters resulted. The newspaper *The Irish Catholic* demanded legislation specifically banning O'Casey's plays. Although the literary and contraceptive censorship was in full swing, the Free State, having got rid of the Lord Chamberlain, had no official censor of theatre, in which condition of freedom we happily remain to this day. The production

of *The Silver Tassie* led eventually to the resignation of Brinsley McNamara from the board of the theatre to be replaced by the writer Frank O'Connor. Together with Sean O'Faoláin, O'Connor had complained of the discourtesy shown by the Abbey to those Irish writers who had submitted work. In this photograph taken in the green-room of the theatre around 1938, the representative of the government on the board, Dr Richard Hayes, for many years Director of the National Library of Ireland, is second on the left.

145

The first production of Lennox Robinson's play *The Bird's Nest*, 12 September 1938. The production by Hugh Hunt with sets designed by Tanya Moïsewitch shows us that the conception had at last got away from the symmetrical box-set, and a simple yet ingenious re-arrangement of flats and furniture makes several radically different viewpoints of the room a

144

feature of the production. Lighting, however, remains primitive. The technical facilities simply were not there to enable any but very simple treatments to be realised. A little over four months later Yeats died at Roquebrune. The board appointed Fred Higgins in his place, but how could such a place be filled? Such men come but occasionally over the centuries.

'Oh all the instruments agree,
The day of his death was a dark, cold day.'

146

The days when loose, unpasteurised milk was sold from solid-rubber-tyred two-wheeled carts carrying milk churns and pint and half-pint measures were begining to draw to a close, at least in the cities. Hughes Brothers, at that time an Irish-owned firm, was one of the first in Ireland to produce bottled, pasteurised milk and to organise its delivery by well designed, horse-drawn milk floats with inflatable rubber tyres. They also produced ice creams which, being made from real cream, were entitled to the precise technical description of 'cream ices'. In those days, January 1939, the milk bottles in use were wide-mouthed and were sealed at the top by wax-impregnated cardboard disks, much tougher for birds to peck through than are the thin aluminium foil caps of taday. Although the drivers had a little more protection from the weather than the drivers of the open carts, they were still much more exposed to it than are the milk lorry drivers of today. They were therefore equipped with waterproof rugs as well as mackintoshes and the horses, too, had their mackintosh sheets. The area manager's modest but efficient small Ford car, the very latest model, is also seen.

145

146

147
A self-fulfilling prophecy in Westport, Co. Mayo, July 1939.

148
Chemist's shop in Dundalk. As well as various proprietary cough mixtures and bottles of cod liver oil, barley-sugar sticks and mothballs, there are several varieties of those devices, now known for their efficacy in promoting oral fixations, the baby 'pacifiers' or 'Silent Soothers'. Iodised table salt, rarely seen in a chemist's shop today, is also for sale. Beside the all-seeing eye at the top is a photograph of the old trestle bridge at Wexford from which local Protestants were thrown into the Slaney, after being piked, in 1798.

148

149

Cork City, 22 August 1939. The ineffectuality of 'A War to End War' was about to be proved, for the second time round, on a really big scale. But in these parts it was to be referred to by that almost cosy euphemism 'the Emergency'.

150

Éire had announced her neutrality, as had the other neutral states of Europe. On 4 September the crew of this Dutch motor-coaster had already painted her neutral designation on her side while waiting to sail from Cork.

151

The balloon had gone up all right. This time there was to be no question of 'peace in our time'. In London, where trenches for shelter had been dug in the parks for a year, there was little doubt among people who had seen the film of H. G. Wells's novel *Things to Come*. It was thought that the next few days or weeks would bring devastating air-raids and mass gas-attacks. Almost everyone now had small, oblong brown cardboard boxes that looked as if they might contain a meagre picnic lunch, but which in fact held rather primitive gas masks with a simple rubber disc non-return valve on the cannister. The exhaled air was supposed to pass out under the rubber of the face mask where the mask lay over the cheeks — which it did with a loud farting noise, if the masks, which came in only three sizes, fitted.

In Ireland, at least in the twenty-six Counties, the atmosphere was more like that in the grandstand at a very important race meeting where there were a great many horses with very long odds. Of course, if one had relatives who were either in the British forces or working in a factory ...

Outside a newsagent's shop, Cork City, 4 September 1939.

149

150

151

152

The Norwegian motor-tanker *Inge Maersk*, also in her neutral colours, noses past Hawlbowline Island in Cork Harbour as she prepares to put to sea in early September 1939. Both Holland and Norway were soon to become occupied countries. The supplies of essential goods and fuel were reduced to a trickle and Ireland would be, for even more years than envisaged at the time, largely dependent on her own resources and resourcefulness. Ireland's hydro-electric power, anthracite, wheat and livestock were to become of vital importance. All of them were commodities that had been the subject of controversy in the past, but now de Valera's policy of self-sufficiency was really about to pay off.

153

The Limerick-owned collier, SS *Kerry Head* alongside the quay at Limerick, on the day after the declaration of war. As Irish coals from the Arigna and Castlecomer mines were, under normal conditions, unsuitable for many purposes, national energy supply depended heavily on coal, mainly Welsh steam coal, imported by small colliers like this one. Unlike this vessel, most were foreign owned and so for the most part diverted to other work schedules. For the early months of the war, these small Irish colliers played an important part in helping to keep supplies coming in. Even though Éire was neutral, her shipping came under attack from German U-boats and aircraft. the *Kerry Head* was the first Irish vessel to be attacked by a submarine, off the Old Head of Kinsale on 1 August 1940. The torpedo exploded at some distance from her hull and she crept into Cork harbour with leaking rivets and was repaired there. On a later trip on 22 October 1940, she was sunk off Clare Island with all hands, twelve in number, mainly Limerickmen but some from Carrickfergus in Northern Ireland.

154

Coal was essential for the operation of the railways, which could take the pressure off the petrol supplies so necessary for road transport. None of the railways were electrified, the only electric service being provided by the Drumm battery-powered train which was only suitable for local journeys.

In this photograph two trains pass on the Dublin-Cork line near Limerick Junction. The oncoming train is hauled by the largest type of steam locomotive ever to run on Irish railways and the last to be designed and constructed here. It is the first of its class, number 800, the *Maeve*, or 4-6-0 with three cylinders and six-foot seven-inch diameter driving wheels, completed at Inchicore in 1939. It continued working throughout the war and, when the Great Southern Railway was taken over by CIE, it hauled the *Enterprise* express between Belfast and Cork in the 1950s. It is seen here on one of its early runs between Cork and Dublin.

155

The driver on the footplate of Great Southern Railways locomotive 406. When originally built for the Great Southern and Western Railway, it was a 4-6-0 with four cylinders, but was rebuilt in a two-cylinder form with Caprotti valve-gear. Instructions for operating can be seen on the wall of the cab. It was men like the one in the photograph who had to coax the locomotives along with unsuitable fuel throughout most of the Emergency.

152

153

154

155

155a

155a
As the thirties drew to a close a unique construction
grew on the north County Dublin landscape at
Collinstown, the site chosen for Dublin airport.
Designed by the architect Desmond FitzGerald, the
terminal building was acclaimed internationally, but it
was little used during the Emergency. However
immediately after the war years it became a focus
popular for family outings and social gatherings at a time
when travel by air was a relatively unusual and
glamorous undertaking.

156

156
During the Emergency, with stringent rationing of
petrol and diesel supplies, even the army made
considerable use of horse transport as may be seen
from these soldiers from the Curragh Camp, Co.
Kildare.

157

157

The wartime conditions were a mixed blessing to Dublin theatre. They made the procurement of materials and the undertaking of ambitious new productions more difficult. But, particularly when the supply of cinema film began to run down, they brought about an increase in audiences. Having no permanent year-round home, mac Liammóir-Edwards Productions found things especially difficult, shifting between the Gate and the Gaiety theatres. In a very intelligent effort to present a different aspect of theatre at no extra cost, Hilton Edwards produced *Hamlet* in modern dress, with a minimum of sets, using lighting in the idiom that he had developed for *Carmilla* and *Liliom*. In spite of having some rather silly press notices, it was an interesting experiment and was revived in the following year.

158

The Spanish Soldier at the Abbey. A new play by Louis D'Alton, it opened on 29 January 1940. It was a vehicle for one stalwart old stager, Michael Dolan, and for two newcomers of importance, Cyril Cusack, seen kneeling and, on the right, Phyllis Ryan.

The National Theatre had also been having its troubles. In 1938, when Yeats had left Ireland with failing health, Fred Higgins became managing director. Towards the end of same year, discouraged by the continual wrangling of the board, Hugh Hunt departed for New York. Frank O'Connor suggested to the board that they appoint the playwright and director Denis Johnston as play director. But their feeling was 'that he would want his own way', as though any play director worth his salt would not! In the event, they gave the responsibility to Louis D'Alton, but he occupied the position for a mere five months and was replaced by Frank Dermody. Barely three months after the opening of *The Spanish Soldier*, Frank O'Connor, feeling 'that mediocrity was in control and against mediocrity there is no appeal', resigned from the board. Less than a year later, Fred Higgins had died and his place had been taken by Ernest Blythe, who became not only managing director, but eventually the majority shareholder of the Irish National Theatre Society Ltd.

159

A net dries aboard a fishing boat alongside the quay at Galway, 22 March 1940. The need for as much food as could be got from the sea made the continuance of fishing important in spite of the risks. In the right background, the old *Dun Aengus* raises steam as she prepares to set out for the Aran Islands. Throughout the Emergency coal was found for her to keep up her link with the islands.

160

In a back street, near the Claddagh, Galway, children play at hopscotch.

158

159

160

161
At the side of a road near Clogher Head, Co. Louth, an itinerant woman and her daughter set up their home in the traditional way of travelling people without a caravan, on 11 May 1940, at 2.16 p.m. Beneath the outer tarpaulin cover, a layer of empty sugar sacks have been placed over the bent stakes to act as thermal insulation. All have now been folded back to air the bedding spread on a tarpaulin groundsheet, as the day is fine. A little dresser has been contrived out of a wooden groceries box, which contains a small amount of crockery and is surmounted by an alarm-clock, a small shrine and a little looking glass. It is interesting to see how shelter from the prevailing wind has determined the selection of the site.

162
Children outside the local National School, Ballinabrannagh, Co. Carlow, June 1940. It is striking that, even in one of the richer counties, seven out of the eleven boys seen are going barefoot.

162

163
The sudden invasion of Belgium and Holland and the collapse of France decided de Valera to bring together in a public meeting in College Green, Dublin, representatives of the Fine Gael, Fianna Fáil and Labour parties. He wanted to make an appeal for unity of effort on the part of the whole country to face the difficult days ahead and a specific call was made for volunteers for the Local Defence Force and other voluntary services as well as for recruits for the regular army.

163

164

The M1 crosses the sheltered waters of Cork Harbour at speed, July 1940. At the start of the war, the Maritime Inscription had a handful of Thorneycroft-built motor torpedo-boats of recent design which had been acquired in 1938. They were built for speed and manoeuvrability, in relatively smooth water, for coastal and port defence. Their chine hulls meant that they were not suitable for operating in the open sea in heavy weather. They were armed with machine guns, torpedo tubes and anti-submarine depth-charges.

165

The largest and oldest Irish naval vessel was a fishery protection boat, the coal-burning steamer *Muir Chú*. She had an interesting history for she had originally been the *Helga*, the British fishery protection vessel which had served in Irish waters. During the 1916 Rising, she had sailed up the Liffey and bombarded the deserted Liberty Hall. Since then she had been extensively refitted. The small calibre quick-firing gun which she had carried, right up in the bows, had been removed and replaced by one of larger calibre, mounted at the after end of the fo'c'sle as seen in this photograph of July 1940. But no thought had been given to the protection of the gun crew who, at this date, were supposed to work the gun in completely open conditions.

164

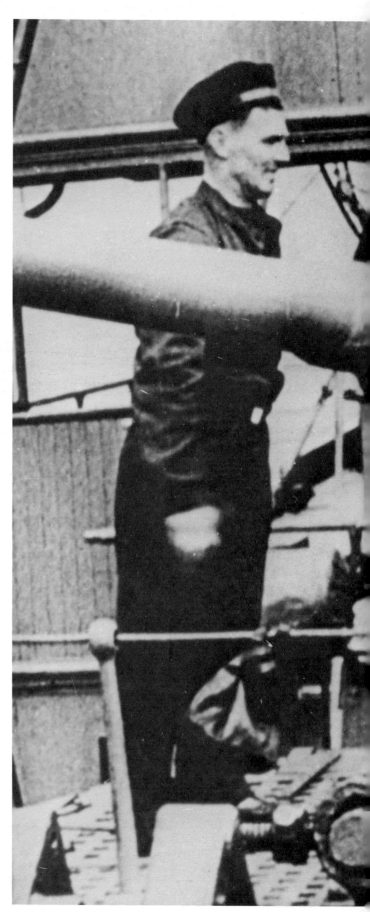

165

166

Similarly, no thought had been given to the exposed condition of the nine-point-two inch wire-wound rifles mounted on Spike Island for the defence of Cork Harbour. They had been constructed in 1902, even before the Wright brothers' first flight, and their mounting a few years later left them totally vulnerable to dive-bombing. They were later to be mounted underground, in casemates, as were the guns at Howth. An interesting feature of the photograph is the small quick-firing gun above and to the left of the main gun.

166

167

Gloster 'Gladiator' pilots of the Air Corps at an open-air briefing at Baldonnel, now Casement aerodrome near Dublin. As well as the 'Gladiators', the Air Corps had a few Westland 'Lysander' high-wing monoplane army co-operation aircraft. There were also several Avro 'Anson' coastal-defence/bombers. As the years passed, the Air Corps added to its aircraft by repairing certain British aircraft that had landed here. Airfields were also defended on the ground by 12 pounder guns.

168

Besides the fighters, which were few in number and out of date, the limited anti-aircraft defences consisted of a small number of 3.7 inch anti-aircraft guns. These were evident principally in the vicinity of Dublin and Cork and their main purpose was to fire off the orange-red star shells that were the recognised neutral-territory signal when a strange aircraft put in an appearance. Besides these there were some Swiss Oerlikons, and a few Swedish Bofors quick-firing anti-aircraft cannon, a clip of ammunition for which is seen being loaded.

167

169

The volunteer Local Defence Force and Slua Muirí were important to security during the Emergency. They acted in support of both the army and the Garda Siochána and had one other vital part to play. In 1922, the Free State government had dispensed with the British Coast Guard watch and communications service and had never formed an Irish one. Now such a service was urgently needed, so the old British Coast Guard observation shelters on strategic coastal hilltops around Ireland were recommissioned, rebuilt and staffed by Slua Muirí and LDF personnel and linked by telephone to command centres.

Here is the one at the top of the hill in Sorrento Park, Dalkey. These shelters had each a small fireplace and chimney where some semblance of warmth and the occasional cup of tea could be a feature of the duty, for, unlike this particular one, some were to be found in very isolated positions.

170

In spite of the superficial impression created by this photograph, the Wehrmacht never landed in Ireland, but one may imagine the confusion which might have resulted had they done so. An Irish Army patrol stops a motorist who has just crossed the Bandon River.

As petrol supplies became tighter, almost all private pleasure motoring ceased. For a brief period a few cars were driven by gas carried in a large rubberised fabric balloon on the roof, but gas rationing and the very short range of this method soon put a stop to this contrivance. Before long only some higher civil servants, medical practitioners, priests and a few agricultural advisors and farmers had a sufficient supply of petrol to enable them to keep on the road in their own vehicles. Electrical engineers in the ESB and engineering personnel of the Irish Lights Commissioners were also a special category; our lighthouses as well as the lights of our cities and towns kept shining.

168

170

169

171
The petrol shortage promoted the continued use of the traditional methods for getting milk supplies to the creameries, although some creameries were now powered from the ESB via step-down transformers. The production of food was one of the priority elements in the Emergency economy.

172

The augmentation of hydro-electric power supplies had a top priority rating and the do-it-yourself self-sufficiency policy of de Valera had helped to prepare the way. The Poulaphouca construction scheme in Co. Wicklow got under way in 1940. Here wooden mouldings are being made for the casting, in reinforced concrete, of the penstocks. Wartime conditions gave a further impetus to the generation of electricity from turf. Every watt of power that could be produced was needed.

173

Although diesel-powered road rollers had made their appearance in Ireland before the war, the real life-savers when it came to road repairs were the old steam-rollers, because they could be entirely maintained and refurbished within the available technology. In extreme cases the skills and special equipment available at the railway locomotive construction works at Inchicore could be called upon. Here a Mayo County Council worker refits the main drive shaft of a steam roller on 11 August 1940.

172

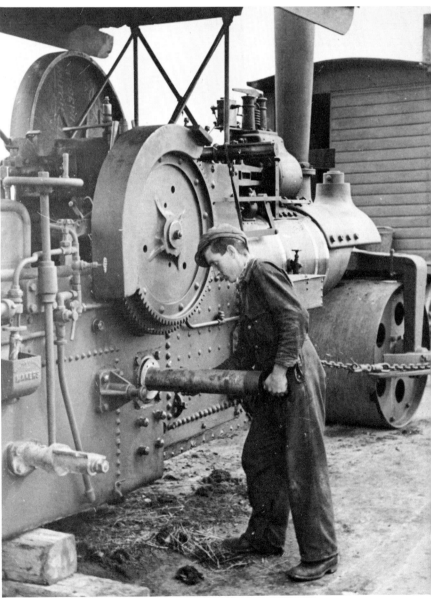

173

In that interesting way in which such events seem often to occur in times of maximum stress, in the grim days of 1940, the most important factor in the renewal of cultural life in Ireland, North and South, was launched by the writer Sean O'Faoláin, in the form of a new magazine *The Bell*. No publication since the founding of the state was to compare with it for the stimulus it gave to intellectual life and to the dispersal of the forces of obscurantism and thought-control that had had things all their own way until then in all the arts, with the single, partial exception of theatre. Since 1929, the provisions of the Censorship of Publications Act had been applied with the active co-operation of the Customs Inspectors, to muzzle, in the twenty-six counties at least, some of the most important work of almost every Irish writer of distinction and international acclaim. The position was rapidly becoming so ludicrous that one man of wide cultural attainments and scientific eminence, Professor William Robert Fearon, had undertaken to serve on the board, in order, as he told the present writer, then one of his students, 'to endeavour to introduce a greater humanity and rationality into its deliberations and decisions if that were possible'. But it was becoming ever more evident that the appalling incubus with which we had saddled ourselves would have to be confronted from without and *The Bell* was to provide a lead and a rallying point for all those who believed in the possibility of a genuinely pluristic cultural structure in Irish life.

In 1941, O'Faoláin took up the defence of a book by the Catholic physician and gynaecologist Halliday Sutherland, the first edition of which had been banned. Called *The Laws of Life*, the book dealt with questions of sexual hygiene and gave information on the calculation of the 'safe' period. Sutherland, in his book *Irish Journey* wrote:

'I believe *Laws of Life* was banned because I had written in the cold language of physiology an account of the function of sex. This could harm no one from the age of puberty upwards. In Éire too many people, including clerics, regard ignorance as synonymous with innocence. These persons should inquire how many Children of Mary from Éire are now prostitutes in Piccadilly.'

175
A fine fair day in Longford town in September 1940. As the Emergency wore on, fewer and fewer private motorists were seen and not many motor lorries either. But there were still plenty of horses and asses and carts. The Great Southern Railways, formed by the compulsory amalgamation of all the railways in the Free State in 1945, had been extending its bus routes over the years. These, though giving a restricted service, were maintained throughout the war and in the difficult years which followed. Here the Longford bus, in its green and white livery, has just arrived.

176 (following pages)
By 1941, with fuel supplies for cars and buses
diminishing fast, the train and the bicycle were in the
ascendant and many train passengers brought their
bicycles with them in the guard's van. Still to be seen
at the right of this photograph of the platform of
Athlone Station is the advertisement for the North
German Lloyd liner service between Cobh and Galway
and New York. But the question of Irish ports was
arising in another context now.

175

Under pressure from the effects of the U-boat blockade, Winston Churchill, now British Prime Minister, was seeking to get Éire into the war on the Allies' side. At the same time studies were made for the invasion of the twenty-six counties, though these were never put into effect. Various forms of pressure were tried — in vain — to influence de Valera to move from his neutral position. On 26 June 1940, proposals were sent to the government in Dublin offering, among other things, a kind of Council of Ireland formed by representatives of both the Belfast and the Dublin administrations, if Éire would abandon neutrality. What the powers of this hypothetical body would be were never clearly defined and de Valera turned down the proposals. As the U-boat campaign built up in 1941, in order to bring further pressure to bear on the Dublin government, the British administration severely reduced the shipping space made available for the transportation of goods destined for Éire. This, together with further losses among the tiny Irish merchant fleet, was bringing about a situation that might seriously destabilise political life in the South. De Valera decided that Frank Aiken, the Minister for Co-ordination of Defensive Measures, should go to the United States to seek to buy ships, essential supplies and defensive arms. The Taoiseach suffered very considerably from the lack of sympathy shown by the United States ambassador in Dublin to Éire's status as a neutral. This did not make Aiken's mission an easy one though he did succeed, after many difficulties, in acquiring two ships for the Irish government-sponsored Irish Shipping Ltd which had been established in March 1941. Others were acquired from among shipping that had taken refuge in Irish ports during the early days of the war and this small Irish merchant fleet did heroic work in keeping essential supplies coming in, despite incurring losses of ships and men.

178
The protected industries of footwear and clothing, antithetical to the principle of free trade though they had been, played a vital role during these difficult years. Waterford schoolboys playing marbles, 5 March 1941.

179
The war had brought about the almost total abandonment of the plans for extensive rural electrification. Electric water pumps did not appear in any numbers throughout the countryside until many years later and simple wells and springs frequently entailed carrying water for long distances in the ubiquitous enamel bucket with the wire and wood handle. Ballydonoghue, Co. Kerry, May 1941.

177

178

179

180
To ensure that articles such as those in the photograph
and other items essential to everyday life and
agricultural use continued to be available, all the scrap
that could be found had to be melted down for re-use.
Here is some awaiting recycling by Irish Steel at
Haulbowline Island, Cork Harbour, in May 1941.

180

181

Of the three Estonian ships that sought refuge in Irish ports at the beginning of the war, two were taken over by Irish Shipping Ltd and helped in the enormously difficult and dangerous task of maintaining exports and imports. The third, SS *Otto*, was not regarded as being suitable. In this photograph of the *Otto* taken in Cork in September 1941, one can see the suspended rings fitted up so that the crew could keep fit by gymnastics.

182

Sheep passing the Treaty Stone at Limerick, on 28 February 1942. They are reminders that food production was one of the most urgent priorities and that intensive efforts had been in progress to persuade farmers in the cattle-raising counties to bring more land under tillage, as wheat was still being imported with increasing difficulty. Sheep could be raised on land where wheat or even oats could not grow.

181

182

183
The Great Southern Railways bus stops at Abbeyfeale on its way to Limerick. The girl has just had her case brought down from the top of the bus by the conductor, who made use of the ladder on the right. The mysterious bundles sewn up in canvas are fresh salmon about to start on their way to hotels in Limerick and Dublin. The bicycle frame shows that British-manufactured articles were still trickling through. The fly-posted sticker on the back of the bus would read in full: 'Give every man his Dew' referring to 'Tullamore Dew' a brand of Irish whiskey.

183A
O'Connell Street, Dublin, on a fine April afternoon in 1942. With only four private cars to be seen in the entire street, the pressure of the fuel shortage is very apparent. The trams, running on Irish generated power, are making an important contribution to the transport problem although the double-decker buses, which had made their appearance before the outbreak of war, will replace them in a very few years. People are beginning to set out from the offices to their homes and the bicycle is much in evidence. In the centre of the street stands one of the concrete and brick air-raid shelters that were an ugly reminder of the times throughout the cities of Ireland.

183

183a

184

The bicycle was the king of the road in these times. In the summer, cycling was extremely pleasant as motor traffic was minimal. It was most important to have a bicycle fitted with a wheel-rim-driven dynamo to run one's lamps, as cycle-lamp batteries, indeed all varieties of battery, were exceedingly hard to come by. But it was an ideal time for making cycle tours. Even at the height of what would normally have been the peak tourist season, accommodation could be readily found in hotels. The photograph shows three touring cyclists as they pass the Central Hotel, Ballybunion, Co. Kerry, in May 1942.

185

The dining-room of the Central Hotel, Ballybunion.
While meat, fish and country butter were fairly
plentiful, the Irish form of the 'National Loaf' was
much darker and much more 'whole-grain', than the
'British Loaf' with masses of bran and husk fragments. It
was best eaten hot from the bakery when, with
plenty of country butter, it was quite delicious. It did
not keep more than a few hours without becoming
very horny and rather sour in taste. Because of the
sugar beet and the sugar factories, one was not too
badly off for sugar if one did not have a very sweet
tooth. The tea situation, however, was truly ludicrous:
one half ounce per person per week! At hotels and
cafes, tea tended to be quite unbelievably weak and
usually 'stewed' in taste. It would not have been too
bad if one could have had it with lemon, but lemons
were not to be had under any circumstances.

186 (following pages)
Tobacco was another bug-bear and one which hit the
smokers hard. Quite reasonably under the
circumstances, it was regarded as inessential and the
quality of all brands of cigarette underwent the
strangest changes which called forth very unfavourable
and sarcastic comment. Pipe smokers were slightly
better off, as their tobacco was a little less degraded,
but their supplies were so reduced and so sporadic that
tobacconists tended to keep what little there was for
favoured customers. Here a 'landed proprietor' is driven
home by his coachman after a visit to his tobacconist
in Kilkenny in 1943.

185

S. W. BOURKE.
CIGAR IMPORTER
FANCY GOODS
PURE VIRGINIA
SWEET AFTON
PURE VIRGINIA
CHURCHMAN'S No1

187

The up train from Dingle emerges onto the main road a little south-west of Tralee, July 1943. Due to deteriorating track condition, which Great Southern Railways did not feel justified in repairing due to decreased traffic density on the line, passenger services ceased on 17 April 1939. The line continued to provide a week-day freight service until 1947. Double-headed working was always essential. The ascent to 680 feet above sea level on gradients which in places were as steep as 1-in-29 meant that a train loaded with cattle needed every ounce of pull that the little locomotives could give. The two seen here are Number 5 (nearest to camera) and Number 8. The former was built as a 2-6-2 tank engine by Hunslet in 1892. It was the only locomotive of that format which worked on the line. Number 8 was a 2-6-0 by the same maker, built in 1910. There were seven other locomotives of this unusual configuration which worked the line in the course of its history. Number 5 is now preserved in the United States.

188

Carrickarnon Customs Post, on the border with Northern Ireland, 1943. Not only had the British made studies of an invasion of Éire; the United States had also done so. This had been taken to the lengths of preparing lists of American servicemen who had living relatives in Éire, making it psychologically more difficult for the Irish army to engage them in combat. Fortunately the necessity for this never arose. But had it done so, it would have been launched from Northern Ireland.

187

188

189

As the fuel position worsened, turf was being used more and more in industrial power generation as well as a domestic fuel. Great ridges of turf, piled twelve and fifteen feet high, extended for miles along the roads in the Phoenix Park, Dublin. Turf being a bulky fuel, these huge dumps had to be renewed constantly and there were not enough freight wagons on the railways for the job. So Great Southern Railways stripped the roofs and interiors of old Victorian six-wheeler passenger coaches and, boarding up the windows and doors, made them into turf wagons such as these seen at Athlone in February 1944

189

Again and again the Emergency demonstrated the importance of self-help and self-sufficiency in the field of basic social needs. But for the economic protectionism that made it possible to establish Solus Teoranta, we would have been unable to produce our own electric lamps at that time when:

> In the nightmare of the dark
> All the dogs of Europe bark,
> While the living nations wait,
> Each sequestered in its hate.

Testing batches of lamps, Corke Abbey, Bray, Co. Wicklow, February 1944.

190

191

192

191
Wartime conditions brought about a great upsurge in what had always been a public health problem in Ireland, the prevalence of both human and bovine tuberculosis. Although some sanatoria had been established on a largely voluntary basis before the First World War, facilities for the treatment of this widespread disease were pitifully old fashioned and inadequate. General hospitals had to admit many more cases for treatment in institutions not specifically designed for the purpose. The day room, Limerick Regional Hospital, October 1944.

The state of health in Éire was such at the end of the war, that in 1945, Fianna Fáil introduced a Health Bill with widespread powers, though the government was to drop it and introduce another in 1947.

192
In spite of the manifold responsibilities which it had overseas, the Irish Red Cross Society began preparation

for the biggest mixed-media event, as we would call it today, that had ever been organised here by a voluntary body. In the spring of 1945, a large public exhibition was mounted as a mass education and fundraising campaign. It was augmented by films and dancers as well as an entirely novel show composed of nearly three hundred lantern slides of cartoon graphics by the artist Eamon Costelloe. They were projected in twenty minutes to a pre-recorded track of dialogue, effects and music — the slide and sound show of twenty years later. The script was written by John Ross. Here performers are recording their parts.

The recordings, which were the first of really high quality sound to be made in Dublin, were by a young English sound recordist of genius who came to settle here, Peter Hunt. His knowledge and techniques were to exercise a big influence on the developing art of sound recording in Ireland. The blankets have been hung up to reduce the reverberation in the room in the Irish Red Cross Society's headquarters where the recording is being made.

193

193

One of the chief purposes of the Red Cross exhibition was to break down the very prevalent public phobia of tuberculosis that caused it to be regarded as though it were a crime, to be hushed up and never referred to or talked about. So ingrained was this mass response in Ireland that a host of euphemistic expressions were in constant use, such as 'her chest is delicate' or 'he has a weak chest'. The subject was almost as taboo as sex. The slide show, called 'Tony Tuberculo', was projected from behind the screen in the Round Room of the Mansion House, as were all the films which were on continuous loop which appeared in openings at appropriate places in the exhibition screens. The larger screen for the slide show was mounted on the Round Room stage and removed when Erina Brady's dancers were performing or when lectures and demonstrations were in progress. Many of Dublin's best graphic designers participated in the exhibition, including the stage designer Carl Bonn.

194

On stage, behind the screen and in total darkness, lay the complex arrangements for giving the show. Two powerful, large format lantern-slide projectors were on either end of the table. In the middle there were two dimmers that would enable fade-ins and fade-outs of picture or, by simultaneous but inverse use, a dissolve from one picture to another. Most of the transitions, however, were made by quickly raising and lowering the paddle-shaped shutters, operated by foot pedals in the centre and giving the effect of an instantaneous cut from one image to another. There was one tricky passage near the beginning of the show where twelve images had to be presented in only five seconds, and the entire thing required a high degree of dexterity and presence of mind by all concerned. At the right, placed on a separate table to avoid vibration, was the

electric turntable and pick-up from which the Simplat discs carrying the sound were played. Once the sound started running everyone had to co-ordinate their operations with it. Quite a change from the tape-controlled slide shows of twenty years later. Left to right: the present writer; projector No. 1, Kevin O'Kelly, whose idea it was; master control, Ernie Gebler, projector No. 2; and, at the separate table on turntable duty, Colm O'Laoghaire. We all seem to have continued our connections with the mass media in later life!

194

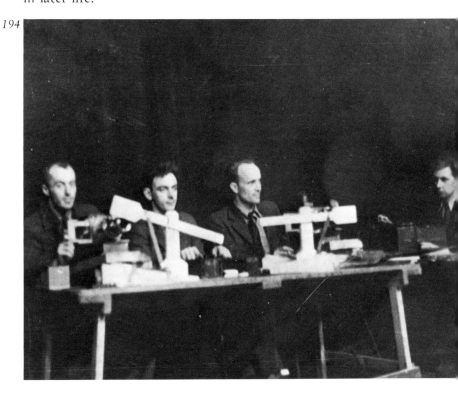

195

195
The old trestle bridge over the Slaney at Wexford, September 1945. From the eighteenth century on, Ireland had a number of these bridges, constructed on wooden trestles supported on wooden piles sunk in the river bed. But for the iron and later steel bolts that held them together, they much resembled the wooden trestle bridges that Julius Caesar had built across the Rhine, and they had been deteriorating progressively for years. When they reached a certain state of decrepitude, a restriction notice forbidding their use by mechanically propelled vehicles would be imposed by the local authority and obstacles erected to prevent motor vehicles from speeding across in defiance of the regulations. As in the case of railway station names and road signs, the name of the bridge was obliterated for the duration of the Emergency.

196

196
From the time of the opening of the transatlantic flying-boat service from Foynes, it had been apparent that with the improvement of aircraft after the war, Ireland would occupy a very strategic position from which to operate services to Canada and the United States using land-based aircraft. The economic advantages of this to the country were evident to the Fianna Fáil administration. Immediately after the end of the war, construction of what was to become one of the most important air communication centres in Europe was put in hand and continued for more than a decade. Though construction work was still going on when this photograph was taken on 29 October 1946, the facilities were busy with transatlantic traffic. In those days Pan American, which had become Pan American World Airways, was using the Lockheed Constellation for its transatlantic flights. One of those graceful machines, with four radial reciprocating engines driving three-bladed feathering airscrews is being loaded with luggage and food prior to take-off. Freedom from obstructions brought about at Rineanna by the wide confluence of the rivers Fergus and Shannon, which is seen beyond the artificial dyke in the background, was one of the reasons for selecting the site. Perhaps one of the most attractive-looking passenger aircraft ever built, more pleasing in line than the Super-Constellation stretched-version that was to replace it, it seemed huge then. But how small it seems today.

197

198

197

Before the war, and apart from the vagaries of weather, flying as a passenger had been a relaxed and elegant experience available only to a travelling elite. One was cosseted and shepherded about as though one were a parcel of the thin-shelled eggs of a very rare and valuable bird. Air pockets during flight, to which aeroplanes and flying-boats responded in a lively fashion, could very rapidly make one feel like an omelette ready for the pan. But, on the ground, all was serene. For a little while after the war, this atmosphere of being in a rather exclusive club persisted and something of it is conveyed in this photograph of the original airside lounge at Shannon Airport on 29 October 1946. And as for the mountains of assorted luggage with which the modern air traveller is familiar, such things were unknown, because there were no conveyors! However one payed for every ounce of baggage above a microscopic allowance in the years before the war.

198

In 1946, the control tower interior presented a vastly different appearance from today. The first impression is one of uncluttered ease: a modest radio-telephone transmitter and a shortwave radio receiver, a chronometer, some telephones and a couple of binoculars, a couple of clipboards of filed flight schedules. Not a sign of a computer terminal, display console, or even a homely tape-recorder. The controller on duty, Robert Howley, speaks to an approaching aircraft. An interesting feature is the installation of fluorescent tube lighting, one of its early uses in Éire. Notice the large size of the starter housing.

199

In place of terminals, computers and display consoles, two very simple devices were in use for keeping track of the relatively low transatlantic traffic density of those days. These were a blackboard and chalk, by which were recorded the aircraft, their call signs and the reports sent in by them of passing through areas of the Atlantic separated by ten degree intervals of longitude. Left to right: C. T. Lonergan, Controller; Michael Manning, Clerical Officer; and Robert Howley, Controller. On the table are seen logbooks and empty schedule forms, and a box of cigars and an ash tray add a human touch.

199

200

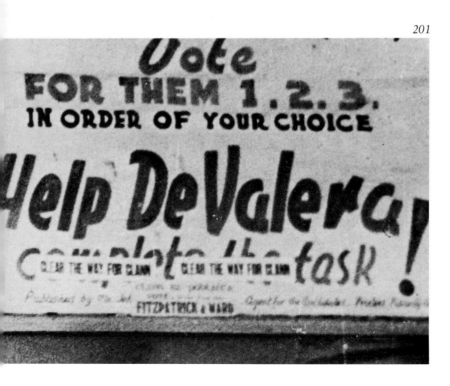

201

200

Following upon the loss of two Fianna Fáil seats in by-elections in October 1947, de Valera called for the dissolution of the Dáil and set the date for a general election in February 1948. The new Health Bill had been passed and had become law, but had not been implemented in any way. Its constitutionality was under test and there had been objections to it from the Catholic Hierarchy, though this was not generally known at the time. Sixteen years of Fianna Fáil administration, the pressures built up from wartime difficulties and the shortages and economic difficulties of the immediate post-war period, a time when de Valera had continued rationing in order to be able to make large donations of food to ease starvation in Europe: all had diminished the appeal of Fianna Fáil to the benefit of other political parties. After sixteen years in office, Fianna Fáil was the only administration that many young people of voting age could remember and they were looking for something new and different. The effective exclusion of the radical left had convinced some of their leaders that the time had come to participate in the elective process and the extremely severe conditions that had obtained during the war in the camps where the more extreme Republicans had been interned led, in 1947, to the establishment of a new political party, Clann na Poblachta.

201

Fly-posting stickers for Clann na Poblachta superimposed on a Fianna Fáil election poster. The new party was led by Sean MacBride, son of the executed leader of 1916 and Madame Maud Gonne MacBride. It had a special appeal to young and radically-minded people who saw in it a way to break the deadlock of what they felt to be a parliamentary structure in Éire consisting of two large conservative parties, one of which would at any one time be in opposition. The publicity for the new party was very ably managed. It made use of modern media technology with specially-made recordings and electioneering films, the latter largely contributed to by Liam O'Leary who directed several lively short films to this end.

202

When the new inter-party Government took office on 18 February 1948, with Clann na Poblachta having ten seats, John A. Costello of Fine Gael was elected Taoiseach — a slightly unusual turn of events as he was not the leader of the Fine Gael Party. The actual party leader was General Mulcahy, but his controversial record during the Civil War meant that he was unacceptable to the redical republicans in Clann na Poblachta, one of the five political parties in the government coalition. Since the government's Dáil majority was very slim, it was essential to avoid any potential dissention. The discussion of cabinet portfolios resulted in two being offered to Clann na Poblachta. Sean MacBride became Minister for External Affairs (as the Depertment of Foreign Affairs was then called) while the Department of Health was offered to a young physician of humanity, talent and drive, Dr Noel Browne, who accepted. The 1947 Health Act, which had become law, appeared to provide a clear instrument for implementing a complete overhaul and improvement of health care in Ireland. In some ways, though not in others, it resembled the extremely extensive National Health scheme in England which, being funded centrally, operated without any form of means test. The proof of the attractiveness of this service to many Irish people was to be seen in the readiness with which they availed of it when in England.

The most urgent problem facing Dr Browne on his assumption of office was the truly dreadful incidence of tuberculosis. It had always been particularly widespread in both town and country because of the amount of poverty, poor housing, malnutrition and a low standard of education which had resulted in general ignorance of its highly infectious nature, particularly in the confined ambience of the family. The first priority was to get the virulently infectious cases removed from the homes, schools and factories where they were a particular menace to the general health in the post-war conditions. An emergency programme of sanatorium building and recruitment of specialist surgeons and nursing staff began at once, using the accumulated capital fund for hospitals generated by the Hospitals Trust. Throughout the entire history of the state there had never been such an energetically pursued initiative as in the campaign against tuberculosis.

202

203

203
Although nothing like those on the Continent, extensive food and fuel shortages still continued in Éire. Shipping space and economic conditions, as well as the need to supply United States grain to the European shambles, made it vital to continue growing as much of our own wheat as the farmers could be persuaded to do. Here, in the autumn of 1948 in Co. Monaghan a reaper and binder are at work — a scene that would not seem out of place a hundred years ago. How odd the stooks of corn look today, while the hedgerows between the fields are thriving. Today the former have almost completely disappeared and the latter are vanishing yearly, to the great disadvantage of much of our wild fauna, particularly songbirds.

204

204
On 18 April 1949, a surprising event took place at the GPO, Dublin. The Taoiseach, John Costello, having abrogated adherence to the External Relations Act, declared the twenty-six counties a Republic, amidst the ceremonial paraphernalia of the usual Easter Parade. The change in status, while nominally approved of by a majority of the inhabitants of Éire, was not to be without complications where relations with Northern Ireland, the status of Éire citizens in the United Kingdom and steps towards the re-unification of Ireland were concerned in years to come.

205
President and Mrs O'Kelly look on during the ceremony. It has been said that Costello took this action due to an experience which he had in Ottawa during a formal dinner of the Law Society. Next to his place at table, he saw a large silver model of the famous cannon which had defended Derry's walls, 'Roaring Meg'. Can sophisticated politicians really act upon such an emotional basis or was there really another reason? In any case the decision to make this important change was not discussed at a full meeting of the cabinet and no trace of it can be found in the cabinet records.

205

206
After nearly half a century of efficient service, the Dublin trams were replaced by Coras Iompair Éireann with British Leyland buses. It has since been suggested that this was not a wise move and that trolley-buses would have been a more rational development at a time when fuel was short and when Ireland could produce considerable quantities of her own electricity. The chassis were supplied by British Leyland while the coachwork was built and finished at Inchicore, Dublin. And the trams? What became of them? Most were scrapped, a few became two-storeyed summer homes and this one, an old Number 15, became 'The New York Hairdressing Saloon' in Loughrea, Co. Galway, where it is seen in February 1950.

206

Dr Noel Browne. By the choice of a scientifically sound strategy, the application of tireless energy and the ability sympathetically to involve collaborators and delegate authority, the anti-tuberculosis scheme had proved, in a surprisingly short time, to be one of the most outstanding administrative successes of any Irish government. The new sanatoria enabled the highly infectious cases to be isolated. The use of the newly available antibiotic streptomycin made dramatic changes in the chances of survival and cure as did the specialised surgical procedures. The widespread introduction of the Baccillus Guerin-Calmette Vaccine treatment helped greatly to lower the incidence of new cases, particularly among the young. It was a unique demonstration of how the right individual in the right place at the right time can stimulate creative social activity to the achievement of a great end.

To appreciate the peculiar fitness of Dr Browne to the task, one must know that he himself came from a very poor family; both his father and mother had died of tuberculosis, as had other members of his family, and he too suffered from it for many years. He had known destitution and the rigours of emigration before the humane attentions of several private individuals secured for him a higher education and, later, enabled

him to undertake the medical course at Trinity College, Dublin. After he qualified, Browne specialised in the treatment of tuberculosis and was for a time on the staff of the sanatorium at Newcastle, Co. Wicklow. With the anti-tuberculosis operation now in full swing, he set himself to the task of implementing the Mother and Child Scheme envisaged in Fianna Fáil's 1947 Health Act. Although that Act only specified a free scheme, without a means test, to give medical care to mothers and their children until the children were sixteen years of age, Dr Browne put before the Cabinet two proposals. One was for a scheme such as the above, without a means test, and an alternative but similar scheme entailed a means test and contributory insurance for those whose incomes were above a specified level.

The Taoiseach asked for a vote as to which scheme should be implemented and the full cabinet, including the Taoiseach, voted unanimously for the implementation of the free scheme, that without the means test. As he had done in the case of the free anti-tuberculosis scheme, Dr Browne went vigorously into action to realise the scheme in practice. There were soon signs that, as distinct from the anti-tuberculosis campaign, certain corporate interests in the medical profession were showing signs of opposition. It appeared too that bad communications within the inter-party cabinet did not reveal at a sufficiently early stage the continuing dissatisfaction with aspects of the Fianna Fáil Health Act of 1947, expressed by the hierarchy of the Irish Catholic Church and left unresolved by the previous administration. Although Dr Browne felt that improper pressure was being exercised by the bishops on the process of parliamentary democracy and cabinet procedure, he made every effort to give the hierarchy an opportunity to put forward evidence of their reasons for opposition to the scheme. But they would only declare that aspects were contrary to Catholic social teaching. They made no attempt to substantiate this claim with evidence of any kind and the cabinet, far from defending their freely taken decision, abandoned their stand. Although Dr Browne had endeavoured to reach an accommodation that would not destroy the medical effectiveness of the scheme, Sean MacBride, with whom his relations had been deteriorating for some time, ordered him to tender his resignation as Minister for Health, which Dr Browne accordingly did. Although a question of inequity of taxation of those who did not wish to take part in the free scheme was one of the objections, this could easily have been met with an opting-out provision for tax relief. The really sensitive issues appear to have been the hierarchy's fear that the scheme would result in sex education, including the subject of contraception, for mothers and for older children. Once again, recalling the Censorship of Publications Act, 1929, and the Halliday Sutherland fracas of 1941, the Dr Browne episode of 1951 reminds one of the famous observation of the great Professor Charcot, in respect of the structure of hysterical neurosis: 'C'est toujours la chose genitale, toujours, toujours, toujours!'

207

a

208

208a

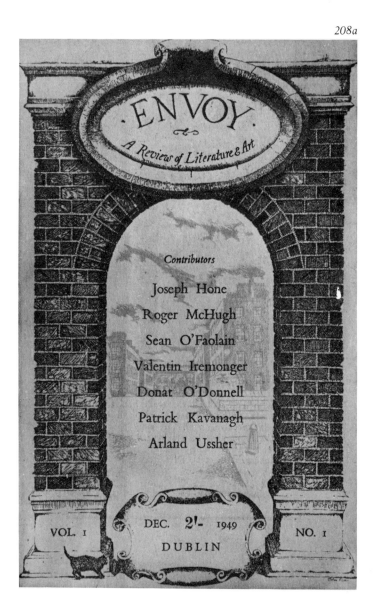

208

In 1949, a young Dublin painter and writer became convinced that Ireland needed a new magazine that would encompass the graphic arts as well as literature. The first number of John Ryan's new monthly appeared in December of that year with a formidable list of contributors and a photographically illustrated article on the work of the painter Daniel O'Neill. Though it did not run for many years, it signalled the breakthrough of the graphic arts into the cultural acceptance that had been, as far as periodicals were concerned, almost exclusive to the field of writing.

209

One of the first innovations of the new administration was the setting up of a semi-state body for which there had been a real need for many years, the Sea Fisheries Board, An Bord Iascaigh Mhara. Irish fishing had never recovered from the changes in the fishing industry that had taken place towards the end of the last century and the beginning of this one; then the introduction of the steam trawlers to the fishing ports of England and Scotland and the availability of rapid rail transport revolutionised the whole structure of fish catching and distribution to the mass markets of the great industrial centres of population. Irish fisheries had languished and decayed and, in spite of the local efforts of Baroness Burdett-Coutts in Baltimore, private investment capital was simply not available on anything like the scale that would have been needed to promote the redevelopment of the industry in the new conditions of the latter half of the twentieth century. The chairmanship of the new board was taken by a man of exceptional imagination, tact and verve, Brendan O'Kelly.

210

Sean MacBride. Further troubles had been undermining the stability and cohesion of Clann na Poblachta. The Minister for Posts and Telegraphs, James Everett, had appointed a friend to the position of Postmaster of Baltinglass, Co. Wicklow, which led to intense local opposition as it breached the accustomed Civil Service procedures and set aside a local candidate. The 'Battle of Baltinglass' became so fierce that the Minister was obliged to bow to the pressure and rescind his decision. Both Dr Browne and Noel Hartnett, who had been the Clann na Poblachta Director of Elections, felt that the position of the party was being compromised, especially when MacBride made an offer of military bases in Éire to President Truman if the latter would intervene in the settlement of the issue of Irish re-unification, mention of which is to be found in the Truman papers. Hartnett resigned from the party in February 1951. On 11 April, Dr Browne resigned both as Minister and as a member of Clann na Poblachta and within a matter of weeks the first inter-party government had fallen. In the ensuing general election, Fianna Fáil was returned without an overall majority and de Valera reconstituted his cabinet on much the same lines as before.

209

210

159

211
As Hugh Hunt expresses it in his invaluable book *The
Abbey, Ireland's National Theatre:*

    'About 1 a.m. on the morning of Wednesday 18 July
    1951, after the curtain had fallen on the last scene of *The
    Plough and the Stars* — a scene in which the fires of
    Dublin's Easter Week are seen through Bessie Burgess's
    attic window — two Dubliners, standing at the corner of
    Abbey Street, noticed a glow in the upper windows of the
    theatre. Suddenly flames shot up into the night sky. The
    Abbey was on fire.'

In spite of the best efforts made by five sections of the
Dublin fire brigade, the theatre could not be saved.
The photograph looks west across the destroyed stage

towards the lighting switchboard at the right of the
picture. It is interesting to see, as late as 1951, what
an exceedingly primitive set of lighting controls was
available in the national theatre. This deficiency was
amply made up in the new theatre which is more fully
equipped than many a television studio and has most
sophisticated controls.

212
At the corner of Marlborough Road and Morehampton
Road, Donnybrook, Dublin, June 1952, is Cyril Fagan,
the internationally famous astrologer, who has
contributed more to that subject than any other writer
in the English language in this century.

213

The climate of the late forties and early fifties had become much more favourable to the development of young Irish writers. In 1946, the absolute autocracy of the Censorship Board had been modified by the establishment of a Board of Appeal. The operation of the Censorship Board in the thirties and early forties had reached a state of absurdity in which all the most serious and distinguished Irish writers as well as hundreds of the best known literary figures in the entire world had come under its interdict. We in Éire had something that can only be described as a kind of literary 'American Prohibition' with the corresponding literary 'speakeasys' where banned books could be obtained by privileged customers. Serious modern literature, however, was failing to get through to the Irish people in general: a really disgraceful state of affairs. The members of the Censorship Board were permanent fixtures throughout their terms of office and for many years the manner in which their successors were selected gave no hope of a more open-minded institution being built up. Although Sean O'Faoláin, in *The Bell* and later Peadar O'Donnell kept up a brisk sniping fire, the institution, in spite of the existence of the Appeals Board, became ever more tyrannical. In the early fifties it banned an average of some six hundred titles every year, both Irish and foreign. Can one wonder that we became the laughing stock of the world, just as the Americans did over Prohibition?

In spite of this and of having their work so frequently banned (which, of course, did them little harm outside Éire) the younger Irish writers were beginning to come into their own in the 1950s. Two poets and a friend have a drink together in Mooney's of Baggot Street Bridge in Dublin. Although they had become embroiled over a law case, the fracas was not to produce a permanent rift between Patrick Kavanagh and Brendan Behan although their outlooks were very nearly as opposed as one could well imagine. This kind of richness of varied viewpoints was what made Dublin literary-pub life so interesting over the years.

213

214

The physics laboratory, Crescent College, Limerick, June 1952. A class in progress. Although the date has passed the halfway mark in the twentieth century, one cannot but be struck by the markedly nineteenth-century atmosphere that prevails. Throughout the thirties, forties and fifties, Éire was remarkably slow to take advantage of the educational facilities that had arisen through the motion-picture arts. There were very few schools that had their own 16 mm projection facilities. Until the foundation of the National Film Institute by Archbishop McQuaid, all educational films had to be brought in on an *ad hoc* basis, and this did much to discourage the use of films in schools throughout the country. Film strips, too, were only just coming into use.

214

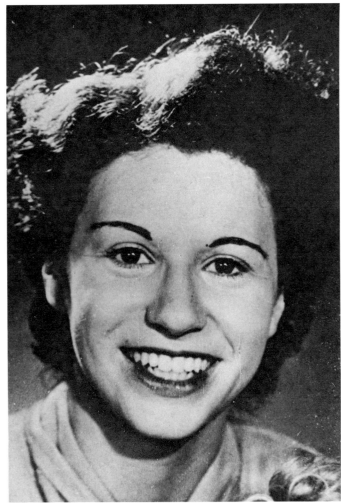

215   215a

215

In 1953, Alan Simpson and his wife Carolyn Swift established the first permanent 'alternative' theatre since the split in the Gate: the Pike Theatre Club in Herbert Lane, Dublin. They opened with the world premiere of *The Surprise* by G. K. Chesterton. Alan Simpson had read engineering in Trinity College, Dublin, and had later spent some years in the Irish Army. When in Trinity he had been a prominent producer in the Dublin University Players and had always cherished the hope that he would be able to make a permanent career in the theatre. From his professional beginning at the Pike he went on to become a producer of note both in Ireland and abroad and played a most salient part, together with his wife, in the struggle for freedom of expression in Irish theatre.

216

After the fire of 1951, the Abbey Theatre leased the Queen's Theatre in Pearse Street and, after a surprisingly short interval, resumed its performances less than six months after the fire. In the Queen's, they had a larger stage and a better lighting system, Here is the première of Louis d'Alton's *This Other Eden*, which opened on 1 June 1953 and was one of the outstanding successes of the season with a twenty-four weeks' run.

216

216a

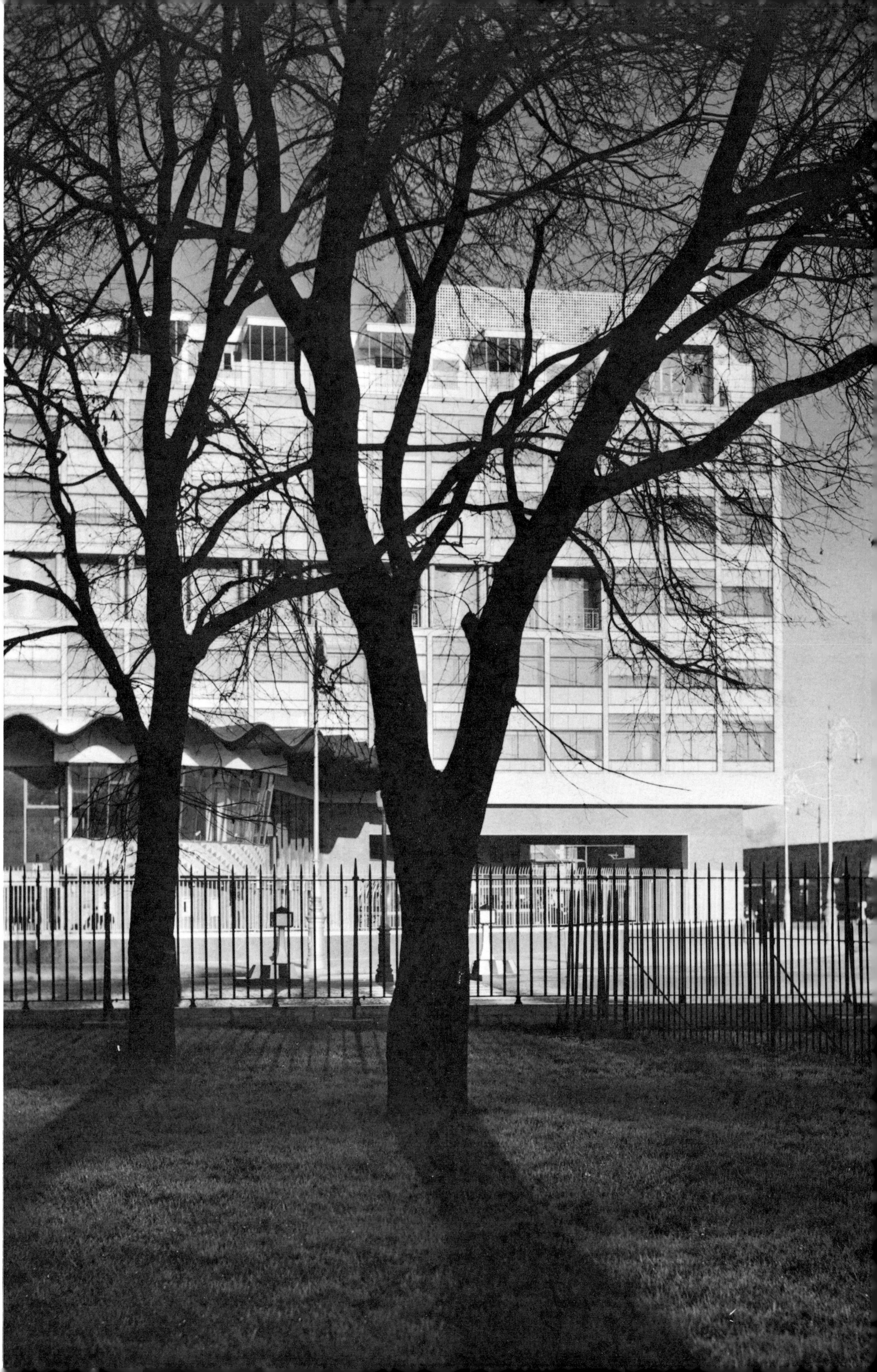

216A
In 1953 the first major contribution to civic architecture was completed by our internationally renowned Dr Michael Scott, who had designed the Irish Pavilion at the New York World's Fair in 1939. The Central Bus Station is a majestic building whose massive structure is lightened and diversified by a series of subtly intermodulated rhythms. Nothing like it had been seen in Ireland before and it aroused much discussion at the time.

217
One of the most distinguished of all our living writers, Samuel Beckett, had suffered almost more than any other at the hands of the Censorship Board and his writing for the theatre had never appeared on any Irish stage. It is hardly surprising that so many of the banned Irish writers chose to live abroad. Here Beckett is seen in 1954 during a brief visit to relatives in Killiney, Co. Dublin.

217

218

218

In the early fifties a new body made its appearance,
one which was to have an important cultural impact
on the Irish scene: Gael Linn. Its purpose was to
promote the use of the Irish language in everyday life
through the sponsorship of art and industry and, later,
by organising competitions and scholarships. It
promoted the work of Irish composers and musicians,
both traditional and symphonic, giving a particular
assistance to Gerard Victory and Sean Ó Riada. They
were also to sponsor a Gaelic newsreel produced by Colm
O'Laoghaire and the films *Mise Éire and Saoirse?* as well
as *An Tine Bheo*. President de Valera is seen here at the
Dublin opening of *Mise Éire*.

218A

Jimmy O'Dea in his most famous comedy creation,
'Biddy Mulligan, the pride of the Coombe'. Ireland's

219

greatest master of comedy in the twentieth century was born in 1899, in the Liberties of Dublin. He had an unerring sense of what most appealed to the Irish sense of humour and, in Harry O'Donovan, found a script writer with a unique feeling for Dublin farce which was to give many decades of pleasure both to Dubliners and overseas visitors.

219
Although James Joyce's *Ulysses* continued to be treated in Éire as literary 'hootch', sold in speak-easy-style and wrapped in plain brown paper, an open rebellion against this kind of idiocy was now in progress. On 16 June 1954 (Bloomsday), a number of culturally distinguished figures from Ireland and abroad assembled to make a perigrination over the route taken by Leopold Bloom in the novel, travelling from place to place in vintage broughams, known colloquially as *growlers*. Here Dr Con Leventhal, author and literary critic and friend of Joyce and Beckett, and Brian O'Nolan, the civil servant who, under the *nome de plume* of Myles na gCopaleen and Flann O'Brien had become a well known writer in Dublin, are about to set out on the journey.

221

220
Radio Éireann having rejected his radio play originally called *The Twisting of Another Rope*, Brendan Behan adapted the work for the stage as *The Quare Fella* and offered it to the Abbey. They likewise turned it down. At this point the importance of having a permanent 'alternative' theatre was seen, for Alan Simpson and Carolyn Swift took it with alacrity and produced it with great success at the Pike. It opened on 19 November 1954 and Brendan Behan was launched on his career as a playwright. Joan Littlewood saw it at the Pike and decided to put it on in London. Two years

223

later the Abbey produced it and have revived both it and *The Hostage* many times since. But in the early days Ernest Blythe's dislike of Behan's work deprived the Abbey of an important theatrical occasion. *The Quare Fella* was eventually made into a black and white film directed by Dreiffus.

221
Another development at the Pike was a series of very popular half-yearly satirical late-night revues with 'Hoddy' — composer, arranger, instrumentalist and musicologist, and now also involved in musical journalism — is the foremost authority on Golden Age jazz in Ireland.

222
So far, neither the Gate nor the Abbey had seen any work by our most internationally acclaimed playwright since O'Casey, Samuel Beckett. Alan Simpson and Carolyn Swift set this right in 1955 when they produced *Waiting for Godot* at the Pike. Produced by Alan Simpson, with Donal Donnelly as Lucky and Nigel FitzGerald as Pozzo, it opened on 28 October.

223
It was during their interregnum in the Queen's Theatre that the Abbey brought to the stage the work of a playwright who was soon to become popular, Hugh Leonard. His comedy, *The Big Birthday*, opened on 23 January 1956.

170

224

Since the war, Aer Lingus had been developing its route network steadily, first to destinations in the United Kingdom and then to major centres on the Continent. This had at first been done with the aid of the reliable and adaptable DC3, but there was now a new generation of aircraft in which the propellors were driven by gas turbines instead of radial reciprocating engines. In 1954 Aer Lingus took delivery of its first Vickers Viscount 700 turbo-prop. In May 1957 the larger Viscount 800 with its extended carrying capacity, longer range and generally improved performance made its appearance. It became the main and highly successful work-horse for the United Kingdom and European network until the introduction of pure jets. An exceedingly comfortable and quiet aircraft, it had delightfully large oval windows.

224

225

In 1958, the year after the introduction of the Viscount 800s, Aer Lingus opened its first transatlantic service between Dublin, Shannon and New York. The company had planned to do this in 1948 and had made preparations, but these were cancelled at the behest of the inter-party government, who were giving priority to housing. Had it been possible for Aer Lingus to enter the transatlantic market at that time, it might have resulted in a sounder structure for the airline on this notoriously difficult route, which was initially operated using Super Constellations on lease from Seaboard and Western Airlines, an American company. The service was extended to Boston later in 1958.

225

On 12 May 1957, Tennesse Williams's outstanding play *The Rose Tattoo* opened at the Pike Theatre, as its contribution to the Dublin International Theatre Festival. Production was by Alan Simpson, with Patrick Nolan and Anna Manahan playing the leading parts. The production received a very encouraging series of reviews from both Irish and overseas reviewers. Gabriel Fallon, for many years theatre critic of *The Standard* and now reviewing for the *Evening Press* said: *The Rose Tattoo* ... is a brilliant example of what today's major playwright can do when he attempts to work in a tragic vein.' Harold Hobson of the *Sunday Times* said: 'I was immediately drawn to the Pike because it is giving the English language European première of *The Rose Tattoo*. It is giving it well. This is a distinguished production, directed with outstanding discrimination by Alan Simpson.'

Suddenly, without any complaints having appeared in the press or at the theatre, on the second Tuesday of the festival the Garda instructed the producer to take the show off the stage. The Simpsons decided that there were no grounds for doing so and, very bravely and with the sympathetic support of the cast, continued to give the planned performances. The next night, amidst a blaze of press photographers' flashbulbs, Alan Simpson was arrested on a summary warrant, as though he were a violent criminal, and incarcerated overnight in the Bridewell. But the undercover organisation that had been responsible for stimulating the police into taking this action had made a serious miscalculation, first of the courage and tenacity of the Simpsons and of the cast and staff of the Pike, and secondly of the fairness, though slowness, of Irish justice. Although the prosecution asked for Alan Simpson to be held in custody, the judge refused this and he was released on bail the following day. The show continued for its full run at the Pike but was unable to transfer to the Gate Theatre as planned because Lord Longford cancelled the contract. The case dragged on for a year with costs rising all the time. In the end, District Justice Cathal O'Flynn refused to send it for trial and in a judgement lasting an hour and a half, he refuted the prosecuting Counsel's statement that the play, as presented, 'outraged public interest, was contrary to public morals and was obscene'. District Justice O'Flynn observed: 'I can only infer that, by arresting the accused the object would be achieved of closing down the play ... It smacks to me of the frontier principle: shoot first and talk after.'

The *Rose Tattoo* episode stands as a landmark in the struggle for freedom in the Irish theatre and is a wonderful example of what a small theatre can achieve, something which a larger theatre with bigger overheads and more complex contractual arrangements might find impossible. Indeed mac Liammóir-Edwards Productions had been leaned on in just this way in 1940, but due to the difficulties of their position and their dependence on leasing other theatres for half the year, they were unable to resist the pressure. In 1958

the entire Dublin International Theatre Festival was reduced to a shambles. Archbishop McQuaid had acceded to the Tostal committee's request for a Votive Mass to mark the opening of the festival. Then he learned that Allan McClelland's interesting stage adaptation of *Ulysses*, called *Bloomsday*, and Sean O'Casey's *The Drums of Father Ned* were to be performed during the festival; according to Hugh Hunt, he had read neither play. Nevertheless, he withdrew his permission for the Votive Mass. This led the organisers, very unwisely, to ask O'Casey to make certain modifications to his play. O'Casey, not one to be intimidated by the belt of an archiepiscopal crozier, retaliated by refusing permission for any of his plays to be performed in Éire, an unhappy situation which lasted for six years.

226a

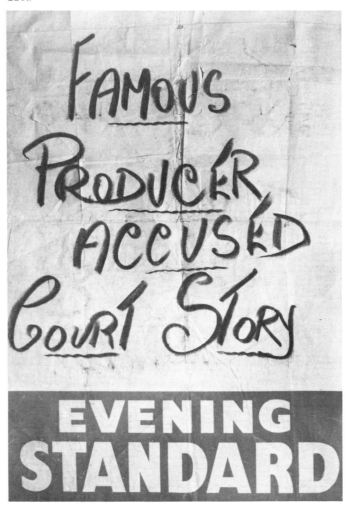

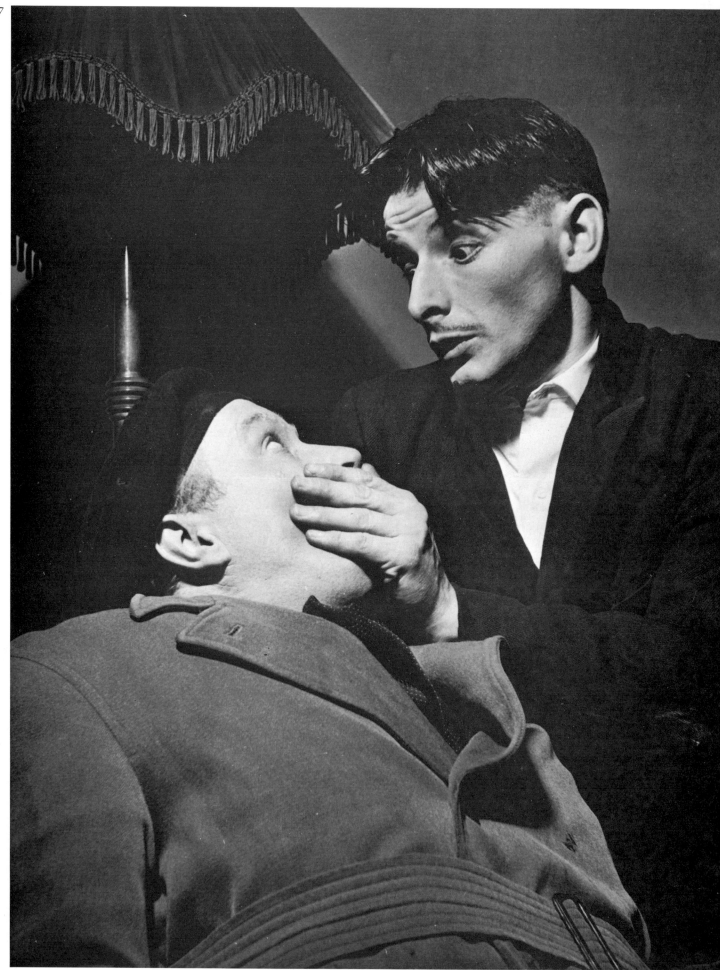

227

In spite of the staggering costs of the prolonged court case, the Pike survived. One of the high spots of 1958 was their production of *Nekrasov* by Jean-Paul Sartre, with Donal Donnelly and Arthur O'Sullivan.

228

In 1959, the then Taoiseach, de Valera, decided to resign from office and stand as a candidate for the Presidency. At the same time and in the same referendum, the Irish people were asked to vote for a constitutional change that would abolish proportional representation as a voting system in general elections. Here is a Fianna Fáil information sheet in which the party sought to persuade the electorate to make the change. When the results of the referendum were to hand, they showed that the people wanted to keep proportional representation but were happy that de Valera should become President.

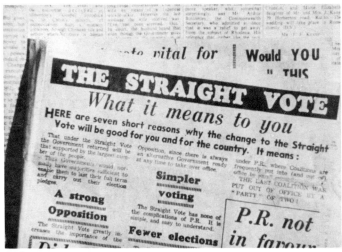

228

229

The retiring President, Sean T. O'Kelly, having received the seals of office from the retiring Taoiseach, presents them to the newly elected Taoiseach, Sean Lemass, at Áras an Uachtaráin on 23 June 1959.

229

230

231

230
Eamon de Valera, on signing the presidential declaration in St Patrick's Hall, Dublin Castle, became President on 25 June 1959.

231
Just before the war, de Valera had established the Institute for Advanced Studies at which the distinguished German physicist Erwin Schrödinger had worked during the war and for some years afterwards. In 1950, under the auspices of the Institute, Cook and Thirlaway had made a gravitational survey of Ireland which was published in 1951. Due to interesting gravitational anomalies revealed by this survey, an increased interest was shown in searching for minerals in Ireland.

232
With Lemass as Taoiseach, greater inducements were offered to foreign firms to set up factories in Ireland, where the continually rising birth rate had been leading to unemployment and emigration. Sometimes, however, the new foreign-owned enterprises did not give as much employment as had been hoped when they got into operation and the foreign ownership led to a steady annual export of capital.

232

233
One of the most successful Irish firms was Roadstone
Limited. From quite small beginnings as quarrymen,
they expanded into one of the biggest suppliers of
ballast and concrete products in the country. Here is
their plant at Ballycorus, Co. Dublin, in 1960, where
gravel is extracted, washed, graded and stored in
hoppers to be carried away by lorries.

234
To provide for the growing electrical demand from
industry, more power stations were needed. The old
plant at the Pigeon House, Dublin, had been in
operation since 1906 and though it had been up-graded
and refurbished a number of times, the ESB decided to
build a new plant at Ringsend, Dublin.

234

235
Building the chimney for the new ESB generating plant at Ringsend, Dublin, 1960.

236
The largest industrial bogs in the world are in the Soviet Union; the second largest are in Ireland and are worked by Bord na Móna. From the beginning, the closest and most cordial contacts were made and maintained between these two publicly-owned enterprises, providing one another with assistance for more than half a century.

During and after the Emergency increasing use was made of turf for the generation of electricity. Here, in 1961, is the production of milled peat for the supply of a large turf-powered generating station.

235

236

236a

237
When it was decided that Radio Éireann should be up-graded into a television service, Michael Scott, the architect who had designed Busáras, the CIE bus station in Dublin and many other fine buildings, was appointed to design it. A then novel feature of his design was the use of pre-cast concrete columns made in a way that resulted in a particularly pleasing surface texture. Here are some of the columns being unmoulded at the Cretestone works, Co. Dublin.

238
The cabling up of the TV studios at Montrose, Donnybrook, Dublin, was one of the most complicated operations of its kind to be done here.

239
Above the large studio at Montrose is the grid from which the pantographs carrying the lights are suspended.

240
Montrose Studios, Donnybrook, Dublin, at once one of the most dignified and graceful yet seemingly light buildings of its kind in the world. Television was to introduce a new cultural epoch, one that would see profound changes in habits of thought and perception.

237

236a
1961 was declared 'Patrician Year' to celebrate the fifteen hundredth anniversary of the birth of St Patrick. It was an exclusively Roman Catholic celebration, for although held in the same year as the opening of the Second Vatican Council, there was no formal participation by any of the Protestant Churches. Here the Papal Legate, Cardinal Agaganian arrives at a ceremony accompanied by Sean Lemass, the Lord Mayor of Dublin, Maurice Dockrell and Archbishop J.C. McQuaid.

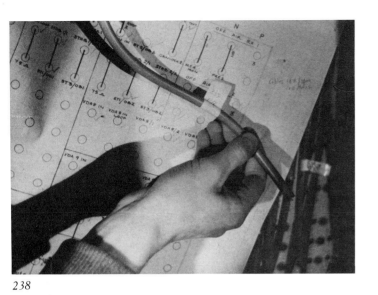

238

239

240

241

242

241
The absence of the Abbey. The site was cleared in 1962 for the foundation of the new building to house the Abbey and Peacock Theatres, designed by Michael Scott.

242
At the opening of the Joyce Museum, the Martello Tower, Sandycove, Dublin. The poet W.R. Rodgers, Seamus Kelly, Sylvia Beach, the original publisher of *Ulysses* who performed the opening, and Michael Scott. 16 June 1962.